Quality of Life

AMERICAN MEDICAL ASSOCIATION

The Middle Years

PUBLISHING SCIENCES GROUP, INC.

Acton, Massachusetts

A Subsidiary of CHC Corporation

The First National Congress on the Quality of Life concerned itself with the period from conception through adolescence. This report of the second Congress deals with the problems, opportunities, and strategies of coping in the middle years — a period of maximum capacity and productivity and yet relatively unknown and uncharted. The Congress was sponsored by the American Medical Association in cooperation with other professional, voluntary, and governmental agencies.

International Standard Book Number: 0-88416-010-6

Library of Congress Catalog Card Number: 73-85402

ACKNOWLEDGMENTS

The American Medical Association is most appreciative of the contributions made to the success of the meeting by the speakers, panelists, consultants, and resource people who shared their expertise with those who attended. We are particularly grateful to the following agencies which cooperated in sponsoring the program:

American Academy of Child Psychiatry
American Academy of Family Physicians
American Academy of Pediatrics
American Association for Comprehensive Health Planning
American Association for Health, Physical Education and Recreation
American Association for Maternal and Child Health, Inc.
American Cancer Society
American College of Nurse Midwives
American College of Obstetricians and Gynecologists
American Dental Association
American Heart Association
American Home Economics Association
American Hospital Association
American Management Association
American Medical Women's Association
American Nurses' Association
American Psychological Association
American Public Health Association
American School Health Association
Brain Research Foundation
Florence Crittenton Association of America, Inc.
Government agencies — federal, state, and local
Joint Commission on Accreditation of Hospitals
Metropolitan Life Insurance Company
National Association for Mental Health
National Congress of Parents and Teachers
National Council for Homemakers — Home Health Aide Services, Inc.
National Council of Churches
National Council on the Aging
National Easter Seal Society for Crippled Children and Adults
National Education Association

National Dental Association
National Foundation-March of Dimes
National Health Council
National Medical Association
National Safety Council
National Society for the Prevention of Blindness
National Tuberculosis and Respiratory Disease Association
National Urban League
Parents Without Partners
Planned Parenthood/World Population
Society for Nutrition Education
Student American Medical Association
Student National Medical Association
United Cerebral Palsy Association, Inc.
Woman's Auxiliary to the American Medical Association
Woman's Auxiliary to the National Medical Association

Ernest B. Howard, MD
Executive Vice President
American Medical Association

CONTENTS

PART ONE

CULTURAL AND PERSONAL VALUES

PART TWO

PARENTHOOD

PART THREE

YEARS OF PRODUCTIVITY AND ACHIEVEMENT

PART FOUR

HUMAN SEXUALITY

PART FIVE

SOCIETAL VALUES AND VALUE CHANGE

APPENDIX

SELECTED PAPERS FROM CONGRESS I

FOREWORD

As a part of its observance of the nation's 200th birthday, the American Medical Association has dedicated itself to improving the quality of life during the bicentennial years and thereafter. The 1972 congress concentrated on improving the quality of life of mothers, infants, children, and youth. This meeting emphasizes the middle years. Congress III, in 1974, will emphasize the importance of making life worth living in the later years.

In sponsoring these meetings, the AMA has elected to serve as an organizational catalyst to increase public awareness of the need for and wisdom of attacking sociological, environmental, educational, and medical problems on an interdisciplinary basis. Just as breath and food and shelter and clothing are the necessary components of life itself, so is the blending of human endeavors essential if we are to be successful in improving the quality of life.

Walter C. Bornemeier, MD
Past President, American Medical Association
Chairman, Congress Planning Committee

PREFACE

Congress II, on improving the quality of life during the middle years, is sponsored by the American Medical Association in cooperation with other professional and voluntary groups and governmental agencies. This congress will concentrate on the social, environmental, and educational aspects of life in the middle years, i.e., early adulthood, mature adulthood, and the transitional years. It is designed to increase the level of public awareness of the importance of the middle years, from 25 through 65, and to stimulate intergroup action on national, regional, state, and local levels.

Because life is complex and coping with its multiple pressures is difficult, improving the quality of life is a major challenge. This challenge demands the attention of all segments of our society. A single congress cannot address itself to the total life-span. Congress I focused on the period from conception through adolescence, because it is during this time that the stage is set for much that follows. These foundation years are crucial if primary prevention is to be realized on a meaningful scale. Congress II focuses on the middle years, for these are the most productive years. They are also an unknown, uncharted period. Research related to this period is not planned carefully, and too often, it is a by-product of other research.

Society makes great demands on people in this age group, and during this period of life, individuals exert great influence on society and make their greatest contributions in terms of family, social, and civic activities. It is imperative that national efforts be directed toward meeting the needs of and improving assistance to these adults in ways that would offer the greatest hope for the future.

Conditions that engender mental, emotional, and physical handicaps for people in the middle years limit individual potential and affect the lives of family and community. Examples of these limiting conditions are lack of identity, lack of maturity, emotional instability, aggressive behavior, suicide, alcoholism, drug abuse, cardiovascular diseases, obesity, and lack of physical fitness. These are complex problems which cannot be prevented or managed by individuals nor by any professional discipline alone. Planned intergroup cooperation is essential in overcoming these problems. Significant efforts have been made by individual agencies to deal with specific problems; however, existing programs are often fragmented and too narrow in scope to reach large numbers of people in need — both affluent and poor. Contributing to this problem is the fact that there is much competition for financing. As a result, human needs are not always met.

Every community must be mobilized for action. This mobilization will require sustained cooperative effort by the private and public sectors at the national, regional, state, and local levels. Business and industry have a big stake in this, because it is the quality of life which determines the economic and political future of our country. An individual's worth to himself, his importance as a contributing member of society, his value as an employee, and his potential as a consumer depend upon and are influenced by his physical and mental well-being.

It is during the middle years that adults work for the orderly growth and development of their children, for happiness for themselves and others, and for effective planning for later life. It will be the aim of this congress to plan ways of overcoming human blight, of nurturing humanness, and of promoting productivity, happiness, and health in the middle years.

PROLOGUE

PROLOGUE

The Quality of Life   **Hugh Downs**
The Middle Years

I can remember thinking as a child that my 21st birthday would be the magical moment when I would cease to be a child, and would simply be an adult, statically, from then on. I did not know the nature of a legal fiction, and I did not then see life as a dynamic flow — a system of becoming. I saw adulthood as a goal. I was to learn later that becoming an adult is not a goal, but rather a mode of travel, a license to improve self, a technique, a process of perhaps limitless scope.

It may be that we are trapped into thinking of adulthood as a goal because one small aspect of maturing does level off in the late teens. We arrive at a suitable height, and then a gland activity ceases, and we don't grow any taller. And this is a good thing — a necessary thing — for muscle efficiency, nutrient availability, and other practical reasons. If average growth rates between the ages of 3 and 18 were to continue, a 75-year-old human would be nearly 20 feet tall. But nothing else in the maturation process levels off in this way. Some things rise and fall and others expand indefinitely.

In examining the potential for maturation in the individual, it is necessary to consider the relative maturity of any social milieu in which an individual may find himself. For this reason I will deal with individual *and* *social* maturity, and with some possible evolutionary directions indicated by a study of maturity.

A human matures in three basic ways: physically, mentally, and emotionally. Physical and mental maturation have characteristic trajectories of growth, peak, and decline. Emotional maturation does not seem to follow this sort of trajectory.

Physical maturing involves growth to an optimum size and strength, development of resistance to disease and the ability to reproduce, maintenance of bodily vigor into and through the prime of life, and afterward a tendency to decline as physical aging sets in and entropy begins to triumph.

Hugh Downs, keynoter of the First National Congress on the Quality of Life and one of the top television personalities of our day, has recently completed a book entitled *Potential* which deals with the maturing man. He also has been working with national and international environmental groups and on television specials.

1

In the first Congress we dealt with the foundation years, from conception to about puberty. Sound physical maturing depends heavily on conditions in these early years. It even depends, as we saw, on conditions before these years, such as the mother's age and health. But if the proper foundation has been provided and proper growth has taken place — if the maturing process has been given good impetus and direction — a sense of physical well-being can persist well into advanced age and will not be eroded by the onset of deterioration. And if emotional maturation is unobstructed, peace of mind will not be upset even in the face of death.

Paul Cunningham, on the *Today* program a few years ago, asked an 85-year-old man how he felt. The man said, "I feel *good*. In fact, I feel as I did when I was 35, as long as I don't *do* what I did when I was 35!" So physical maturation *can* admit an increase of comfort if limitations are accepted without anxiety and if the self is balanced.

Mental maturation follows somewhat the same trajectory, but if maximum mental efficiency is reached at about 28, mental ability can actually improve after that age because of acquired techniques and accumulated wisdom. However, mental processes are also eventually brought down in the ruin of the physical vehicle.

Emotional maturation is a different breed of cat. Long lists of experts have stressed the ability to love as the main characteristic of emotional normalcy and health. The ability to love means to give unconditional love, not to *make* love or to be loved or to indulge jealousy, possessiveness, neurotic dependency, or sadistic control or any of the trappings that accompany literature and myth on the subject. Erich Fromm and Allan Fromme, Theodor Reik, and Wilhelm Reich, along with other popularizers, have written whole books on the subject, the gist of which is that the ability to love is characteristic of the mature person.

Freud said that a normal person should be able to love and work. Other physicians would add play to these two activities. Still another, Richard Cabot, listed love, work, play, and worship as the activities a healthy person lives by. More detailed criteria from psychologists include such qualities as character and integrity. Frank Barron adds effective organization of work toward goals, correct perception of reality, and interpersonal and intrapersonal adjustment. A. H. Maslow lists these attributes: more comfortable relations with reality; acceptance of self, others, and nature; spontaneity; problem centering; detachment (in the need for privacy and in the sense that friendships and family attachments should not be clinging, intrusive, and possessive); independence of culture and environment; continued freshness of appreciation; limitless horizons; social feeling; deep but selective social relationships; democratic character structure (that is, respect for any human being just because he is human); ethical certainty; an unhostile sense of humor; and creativeness.

As the list becomes more detailed, each characteristic is seen, if looked at closely, to fit into the first two broad categories: love and work. If we are permitted to define love and work in really broad but not unreasonable ways, we find there is really nothing else. "Effective organization of work toward goals" is part of the definition of work, when we consider work in human terms and not just as production of foot-pounds of energy. "Character and integrity in the ethical sense" is part of love. And so it all boils down to love and work.

Even play and worship are subordinate. Play is an attractive thing, although I believe it is not a necessity for a highly mature person. To list "to be able to play" as an attribute of full maturity is to miss the point of maturity. It is like saying "to be able to take aspirin" or "to be able to stay sober." In a community where headache is universal, to be able to take aspirin would be a plus, but if headache could be done away with by diet change and fresher air to breathe or by general enhancement of health, then aspirin would not be a factor in well-being. I think the same is true of play and worship, and in an ideally mature society they might vanish. At least they would remain only in the sense that all work would be flavored with play and all living — every moment — would be flavored with worship. What would vanish would be recreation and religious ritual.

It may be that we've gone astray in our civilization by imagining the productive years of drudgery. We should never have separated work from pleasure. Someone once said, "Find pleasure in your work, or you won't find pleasure." And this is the part of the work ethic that I'll defend to the last breath: there is no lasting happiness or satisfaction apart from commitment and effort. These are so much a component of pleasure that the futility of seeking happiness through passive acceptance should be immediately apparent. The idea that you can be happy lying under a bread-fruit tree while nourishment drops into your mouth is a deadly lie. We must commit ourselves, we *must* remain vulnerable, we *must* work, we must grow up enough to love it, or life becomes empty.

The Puritan ethic that deferred reward and equated work with drudgery has bred a lot of mischief. It led to a concept of retirement that is appalling: drudge your way through the work years till you're 65 and then sit on the porch and die earlier than necessary because you're useless. But we'll deal with that at the next Congress.

The Puritan ethic is not the work ethic, although I fear they are often confused. The Puritan outlook demands that you work and be miserable, with the understanding that you'll be rewarded in heaven. The work ethic asserts simply that to be happy you must commit yourself to something you believe and expend effort in its behalf — and learn to love what you are doing. It can be done, and it mitigates the considerable burdens and stresses of the middle years.

THE INDIVIDUAL AND MATURATION

The newborn infant, for all he has to learn, brings with him a number of processes and systems already honed up, such as postdigestive utilization of nutrition, cell division and differentiation, blood circulation, and a functioning network of sensory and motor nerves coupled to muscles that have been given a few brief trial runs before birth. But whole systems are thrust into action at birth, or soon after, which have developed with no trial use — among them the respiratory and digestive apparatus. The sudden shift from potential to kinetic would make it seem to the newborn that this new environment is an inferno, except that he brings no concept of an inferno with him. He is intensely aware. His mind is a great blank territory registering experiences in their purest form, uncluttered with labels, unencrusted with the barnacles of past impression or the prejudices of cultural conditioning. There is no past. He is starting *now*. And his mind is so virginal that he is, in a sense, identical with his awareness of all that's going on within and without. He has not as yet adopted the convention that his skin forms a boundary that separates him from the rest of the universe, nor has he found the emotional parallel — an idea of ego that will tend to *isolate* him from the rest of the world.

His education is about to begin. He is about to start learning names and games, dos and don'ts, musts and oughts, goods and bads — all useful for relating to other beings and for manipulating and exploiting his environment, of which he is at the moment an undifferentiated part. These names and games are useful fictions, and if he were born into a culture that would help him avoid confusing the games with the realities, he would form a sort of ego net, through which he could deploy tentacles for constant empathetic interaction with the world as he grows in the flow of its, and his, becoming.

But there is no such culture in the world. So instead of forming an ego *net*, our newborn human will callous himself against almost continuous trauma, will gradually weave around himself a sort of fibrous casing, tough, perhaps translucent like the cataracts on old eyes, with few interstices and with little capacity for indefinite growth. It will take some years to complete this cocoon, the inside of which may contain some reflective surfaces, in which he will see himself; he will entangle that view with the distorted information coming through from outside.

This is the lot of almost all humans. A few manage to build an interior organization efficient enough to enable them to put some energy to the task of cutting windows in this casing, through which they can see things as they really are and through which they may reach to participate. A very few may knock out whole walls in order to live outdoors, so to speak, and a small handful have apparently managed to abandon the structure of ego entirely to become wanderers under the infinite sky. These are the sages. According to stories about these people, and as nearly as we can understand or interpret the accounts, they share these points in common:

1. They suffer no thwarted desires and no fears, and they appear to sustain a positive happiness.
2. They are awakened to some kind of heightened consciousness.
3. They find and proclaim the world to be unspeakably beautiful.

4. They regard time in a manner that renders each moment eternal.
5. They consider the personality as separate from and transcending the individual ego, which they regard as a fiction anyway. This attitude gives them an identity with the universe and some kind of immortality.
6. They tout no irrational miracles and they preach no doctrines of self-denial or sin or transcendental godhead.
7. They claim no special divinity and regard every human as possessing the capacity to attain this height.

This degree of expansiveness appears to approach something so much more abiding than organic existence that it would be unlikely to suffer reversal through physical deterioration. This is one of the things that gives emotional maturity an apparent exemption from the growth-peak-decline trajectory.

W. H. Cowley says that mature or integrated people are not "adjusted" people: "They are people who are intelligently going about the work of ordering life and harmonizing it on an ever higher scale of human excellence. They are not conformists; they are reconstructionists." Adapting and conforming in the mature person are not compulsive. Adjustment can be consciously used. It is not automatically needed, nor is it habitually avoided; avoidance can be compulsive, also. Child psychologist James Plant puts it this way: "Life is not so much a matter of the adjustment (to) problems, but one of the *adjustment to having problems.*" One can be selective about conforming.

The self-actualizing aspect of this interpretation of conformity came late to psychoanalytic theory. There is much determinism in Freud's original view of the ego caught between two tyrants — the superego (a conditioned conscience) and the id (raw animal drives). Little room was left for a creative force to impel the individual toward ever higher maturity. Freud's ego could at best maintain a shaky balance — an uneasy truce between these powers that pressed on it. Gordon Allport sought a way out of the dilemma by proposing an ego-ideal.

> Certainly a man is not mature unless he respects the codes of the society wherein he lives, acts with good taste and abides by the laws, suffering pangs of conscience when he violates the rights of others and when remiss in his prescribed duties. But is this activity of the Super-Ego all there is to the "higher nature" of a man? Left to itself the Super-Ego would produce a personality completely caked with custom and shackled by tribal mores. Conventionality is not the same as maturity.

Again we see room to be selective about conforming. Since this is self-actualizing, it is creative. Since it is creative, it relates to work. Creation is work — the best kind. And since creativity and love are interlocked on several levels, we see the relationship between love and work, Freud's two verbs that belong to the normal human.

Let's talk about love.

Sometimes the only way to avoid the taint of cliché is to plunge squarely into a nest of clichés, look around, sort them out, and see if some aren't still useful. Whenever we speak of love, we open the door to imprecision so wide that any disciplined system of investigation shivers and runs. The very word "love" is a great semantic bog, but I don't think anybody doubts the existence of love. In yesterday's scientific beliefs, there were such things as phlogiston and caloric fluid and ether, and they are all gone because they never existed to begin with. But love, however confusing, however embarrassing to logical tidiness, is something we all know really exists. Maybe it can never be "dealt with." Maybe it can only be experienced.

Much that passes for love in fiction, tradition, and social concept has nothing to do with love. Jealousy, possessiveness, sexual hunger, sadistic control, conditional affection ("I will love you *if*"), neurotic dependency — none of these is love or a component of love.

The mature person loves beyond need. "Being loved" has its gratifications, but to set about loving in order to be loved in return is futile. The nature of love does not allow it to be employed as a means to any end: "Love isn't love till you give it away." The outward quality of love illustrates its kinship to the same infinite series of processes that characterize understanding. It might be noted that volition has the same property. Einstein commented on this in a discussion of free will and determinism: "I will to light my pipe. But what is behind the will? Volition." And something not named is behind volition. And if we tag that something, there will be something behind that, and so on. When we realize that there is no end to such a process, it dawns on us that this can't be labeled — anything we enclose in a concept and label with a name is stamped with the limitations of human thinking: The ocean, to a five-gallon bucket, is five gallons. Love, too, removes itself step by step from the confinement of identity by either a label or an ego. It will not be confined. And when it is pursued, it recedes again.

The aware person is one who has quit trying to see the stars by building more signal fires. The mature person understands and loves; he doesn't pursue or possess.

It is difficult to understand the connection between loving one other person and loving one's fellow man. When a person, as love object, becomes the focal point of romantic or obsessive feeling, this emotional turn often entails specific exclusion of anyone else. That is part of the nature of love, it seems.

I believe we have to be very suspicious of this exclusivity factor. When desire and romantic feelings focus on one person, it is certainly "natural" because nature, at least in heterosexual relationships, fixed it this way so that there is a maximum likelihood that reproduction will result from the liaison. Being together is more likely when romantic feelings are added to mere sexual hunger, which is always more transitory, and being together over a period of time maximizes chances of impregnation. Nature utilizes and shapes the elements of love for the purpose of perpetuating life. There is nothing wrong, and certainly nothing unnatural, in the process or in enjoying it when it comes to us, but it would be a mistake to imagine that this is the totality of love.

The popular belief concerning the relationship between romantic love and love of humanity, or generic love, seems to be that the wider caring for all of humanity is a transformation — perhaps a perversion — of the more "natural" drive to love one person. The reverse is true: Love is limitless, and while a portion of it can be grabbed and used by biological urge to illuminate and ennoble a fundamentally sexual relationship, it is a mistake to think that this is all there is to love.

So generic love is not merely a transformation or sublimation of romantic love any more than is parental or filial love or kin feeling or deep affection for a venerable pet or a class of endangered wild animals. There are many kinds of love. And because some of them literally have roots in instinct, we can infer that it is *within our nature* as mature personalities to care.

SOCIAL STRUCTURE AND MATURATION

The ancients felt that man had to rise above his nature. Puritans felt this way, too. But modern individuals feel it is *within* the nature of humans to progress to maturity. Intellect has provided the tools to progress meaningfully. But intellect has also sharpened our competitive instincts.

In the necessary transition from competition to cooperation in human society the question arises, will we continue to compete, to hate, to struggle, since we evolved from a world in which we would simply have perished without competitive instinct? And is it normal and natural for us to leave undeveloped the capacity for love and affirmation of life that we apparently possess? Or does the failure to cultivate this potential offer evidence of illness? Psychiatrist G. B. Chisholm, writing in the *Survey Graphic* (1947), said:

> The difficulty man has with himself is that he can not use his highly developed intellect effectively because of his neurotic fears, his prejudices, his fanaticisms, his unreasoning hates, his equally unreasoning devotions; in fact, his failure to reach emotional maturity, or mental health.

Here is a psychiatric view that failure to reach the potential is illness.

Under the pressure of the dangers posed by the enormous weapons capability of the world's nations, the need is present and strong to develop a different kind of human — a human able to grow up and leave behind the destructive instincts of an evolutionary past and develop fully the cooperative faculties that appear to be present in some embryonic form in the psyche. It is not unreasonable to assume that if maturing is within our nature, then techniques for achieving some level of maturity should be available from within, and it is more a matter of discovering than developing them. I think this is true. Maturing is natural, in this sense.

Let's deal for a moment with a gnawing doubt, a doubt that says, "How certain can we be that effort of any kind can increase the percentage of people who mature? Might it not be a fixed statistical sprinkling that no amount of education, or cultural security, or psychological technique can increase?" To my knowledge there is no authoritative proof that this might not be the case. A society could conceivably be highly and widely educated without any increase in the proportion of citizens enlightened with the insights that attend and characterize maturity.

Without such proof I can only advance reasons for behaving as though such an increase is possible. I am assuming that human life has a meaning of some sort, or that it can find or create one; that it is desirable that human life continue, not necessarily unchanged; and that there is such a thing as relative maturity, however imprecisely defined. I further add as informal hypotheses that human societies requiring (and contributing to) maturity of their citizens are structurable and that they already exist, on a relative scale; that ever greater numbers of mature citizens will, through their societies, direct human knowledge to greater human good; and finally, that this greater human good will promote evolution — not Darwinian evolution, but the broader process of which natural selection is a part, the evolution that leads from blind chance to competitive force to cooperating mind, with increasing complexity of organization and levels of consciousness at each of several thresholds.

If the percentage of people in a society who can mature *is* a fixed ratio and if that ratio is impervious to the pressure of any human institution or technique, then the breakthrough may come from some oblique quarter. It may come simply from an environment saturated with information, whether or not the information is formally educational in nature. And of course it may not come at all. But in the absence of proof, let us simply *assume* that it will be worthwhile to research the problems and promises of the middle years — years in which there are so many moments of stress and opportunity and learning potential. The satisfactions may lie in the establishment and reinforcement of purpose so badly needed now by mankind, the opening of the channels to personal maturity, which are usually clogged by a society's demand for conformity and allegiance; the awakening of man to the compatibility of personal interest and social good; and the reduction and eventual elimination of the waste and agony of emotional darkness.

The existence of these congresses justifies my optimism. Planned intergroup cooperation is a necessity, and here we have the preliminary planning for just such interdisciplinary action. Physicians alone can't bring about what we desire here, any more than legislators alone, or policemen alone, or educators alone can do so. Dr. Roderic Gorney will speak later in the proceedings about the human agenda. We have to strive not only for what we want, but we must also order and articulate what we want. We aren't quite together on that. At the moment, the rallying point may not be so much a conscious feeling of the need to mature, as an overwhelming sense of the wrong of wasting human resources.

I deeply believe that there is in every human a potential for maturing. Whether or not we have the skills at present to allow and help everyone to mature, the possibility remains with everyone. Nature does not endow life forms with characteristics that are not capable of fruition under certain circumstances. In light of the past course of evolution, there is every indication that something will unlock the human urge to move ahead. The happiest individuals in the next generations will be those who feel they are contributing to the effort.

Discussion

MODERATOR

Hugh Downs, keynoter of the First National Congress on the Quality of Life and one of the top television personalities of our day.

PANELISTS

Pauline B. Bart, PhD, associate professor of sociology in psychology, Abraham Lincoln School of Medicine, University of Illinois.

Erwin A. France, administrative assistant to Chicago's Mayor Richard J. Daley and director of the Model Cities-Chicago Committee on Urban Opportunity.

John R. Hogness, MD, president, Institute of Medicine of the National Academy of Sciences.

Duane J. Mattheis, PhD, deputy commissioner of school systems in the U. S. Department of Health, Education, and Welfare's Office of Education.

James G. Price, MD, president, American Academy of Family Physicians in 1973.

DEFINITION OF THE QUALITY OF LIFE

Mr. France: We have to talk about the quality of life, and about improving the quality of life, because we have to acknowledge the fact that there is a great disparity between what we expect in the middle years and what many of our citizens experience. We can't define quality of life with great precision, but we can build a working definition. People ought to have jobs, they ought to be healthy, they ought to be able to support their families, they ought to be able to enjoy many of the amenities of life, they ought to get quality education, and they ought to be able to make constructive use of their leisure time — with the widest possible range of options available to them.

Dr. Hogness: As we go along, we also have to decide what we want to do to improve whatever we mean by the quality of life. Then we have to ask ourselves whether we have accomplished that.

Mr. Downs: The problem is to quantify quality. For any scientific inquiry, there has to be some measurable approach.

Dr. Hogness: It gets to be a very practical problem, because sooner or later one goes to government to ask for support in improving the quality of life.

The government wants to know what you mean by that and how you're going to prove that you're doing it once you've got the money.

Mr. France: That's a valid point, but I think it can be overstated. We know when a baby is born with brain damage and when he isn't. I don't know how you quantify that — maybe in terms of numbers of births — a reduction in the number of babies born with brain damage or a reduction in infant mortality. But it seems to me that there are some qualitative elements that do not lend themselves to quantification. We ought not get so hung up on the question of quantifying that we miss the point.

Comment: The thing that concerns me about physical, mental, and emotional health is that we really do cop out on setting up criteria for those. We really don't say what constitutes quality of life in any of those. Why can't we deal with quantifying? What are the minimums at any rate?

Mr. France: While I don't think we can quantify, there should be certain minimum standards. One of the things that concerns me greatly is what appears to be a reversal of national priorities in using federal resources to deal with the problems of the poor and the disadvantaged — the people who find a great disparity between their lives and what is seen as the American norm. Most of us also know that significant segments of our population — and they are not all black incidentally, because two-thirds of the poor population of this nation is white — are falling below the lowest income level that can secure their minimum needs. Yet the President said on television that the urban crisis is over. I don't understand that when I see so many people still living below the poverty level.

Dr. Hogness: I agree wholeheartedly. It is not very obvious what the minimal standards are in all the areas that we are concerned with, but we must start defining those minimal standards of in housing and in health and in environment, and so on. Much of the job of definition can be done.

Comment: We shouldn't stop at simply defining it either. We should take action and use our expertise and our access to skills and to the media to bring about a change in the climate of opinion.

INTERDISCIPLINARY APPROACH

Mr. Downs: Each answer that is given points up the need for an attack on these problems from several directions at once. What is the prognosis for the success of interdisciplinary and intergroup work that will move us toward solutions?

Mr. France: I'm not sure I have a prognosis, but I think we'll have little success until we stop taking certain things for granted. For example, we talk about improving the quality of life as though that is unquestionably a good thing to do, without taking into account the negative aspects of upward mobility — the fact that as we intervene in the lives of people, no matter what discipline we come from, we create certain problems with which they then have to cope. And in many instances these may be greater problems than the ones they brought to us.

This is particularly true of our dealings with the poor and the disadvantaged, who in some respects have to be set apart from other populations — particularly when we are talking about the middle years — because many of them approach their middle years ill-equipped, having been ill-equipped in their earlier years. And if you believe in the developmental task concept, then you have to assume that there is no reason to believe that intervention at that point is necessarily going to help them come to terms with their problems quickly.

I think we at least ought to acknowledge that there are some very special problems involved in trying to help people make life better for themselves that in many instances exacerbate the problems they bring to us.

Mr. Downs: How do you assess the relative harm? I got a more or less firsthand glimpse of the results of an effort to improve the quality of life during the production of a television special on the Eskimo people. It was my conclusion that the governments of Greenland, Canada, and the United States have conscientiously attempted to help these people. The alternative would be to tell them to go on hunting with stones and spears and living in igloos even though other alternatives are available to the rest of us. How can we work our way out of this problem of doing harm when we really intend to do good?

Dr. Mattheis: Let me give you an example. By opening up avenues in education, we have exposed the subsequent problem of employer resistance to disadvantaged minorities with new educational skills. And that's a real problem. We have approached it by working very closely, and I think quite successfully in recent years, with such groups as the labor unions in breaking down unrealistic qualifications and in having them participate in the training programs.

Because there is going to be an ultimate problem, it shouldn't prevent us from starting down the road. It is a challenge, but we should not forgo the first step because we think there is some harm around the corner.

Mr. France: We can be conscientious and at the same time inept, and the real question becomes one of identifying the range of resources with which we are dealing. And how do we integrate them so that we get maximum service from them to produce the best possible result? There still may be some harm done after all that.

Dr. Bart: As professionals and as scholars, we need a certain dose of humility. We should not assume that our ways of doing things and our perspectives are superior because we all have limited perspectives. We all see certain things and are blind to other things. I think our function is to point out various techniques, to point out alternative ways, and then to give the individuals and the groups with whom we deal the choice to use them and give them strength. This approach could decrease the alienation so many of these people feel and could reduce the harm we do.

Dr. Price: Maybe what we're talking about is allowing the individual the choice to decide what quality his life will have. Let me tell you why I say that. About 20 miles south of my home out on the plains of Colorado, there is no water and no irrigation — just sand hills, sagebrush, and cactus. I went out there recently to see a patient. There's a one-room sod house, a couple of scrawny chickens in the front yard, an iron hand pump, and some barbed wire fences. And as I came into the yard, the lady of the house, who is about 50, walked out, yawned, stretched, looked around, and said, "God, isn't it beautiful. Ain't life grand." Her life had a quality that we don't want to tinker with — especially in view of the fact that a quarter of a mile behind her house, three oil wells were pumping. And she had what she wanted. Let's allow people a choice, within reason.

Mr. France: But I think that as we do that, we've got to offer a range of options. Ignorance could have produced that same result. Part of our task is to identify for people the widest range of options and then let them make choices.

Dr. Price: We can't do nothing just because we're afraid that what we do may not be totally right — and this applies not only to doing nothing to improve society in general or the life of any individual, but also to doing nothing because an individual may not know what is possible and therefore does not ask for anything more. We can show historically that we are doing better in terms of the quality of life, and there is every reason to think that we should be able to do even better as we become more sophisticated.

I think the interdisciplinary approach to the solution of these problems we're discussing does in fact give us some guarantee that we will be doing more good than harm. If you turn one profession loose on a problem that is so complex the professional himself doesn't totally understand it, you run a risk.

Mr. France: I would like to underscore the importance of an interdisciplinary approach, but I also want to be sure that my earlier observations didn't get skewed in the wrong direction. The observation I made with respect to the problems created by the introduction of certain stimuli was not meant to suggest that we balance value judgments of the need for accomplishment against the avoidance of doing harm as much as it was to suggest that we need to be prepared for the side effects as well as the treatment, so to speak.

Comment: Can we do more through groups or on a one-to-one basis? I feel, through personal experience, that you are less likely to do harm on a one-to-one basis.

Dr. Bart: The social-psychological support of groups is very, very powerful. They are more powerful in many instances than individuals, which means

14

they are more powerful to do good, and they are more powerful to do harm. To bring about changes, we have found that some of the most useful tools are group tools. For example, one of the most useful ways of fighting alcoholism is not through individual counseling but through such organizations as Alcoholics Anonymous. Similarly with drug treatment programs. Similarly with the various liberation movements that have given various groups in our society a new sense of self-love and self-confidence.

Mr. France: It seems to me that you cannot look at it entirely in terms of professional practice. The fact is that everybody born into this world, at least until he dies, is affected by all kinds of organizations, institutions, and agencies. So the group influence is there. I would say that groups, from the family to the social agency, probably exercise a much greater influence in the lives of people than individuals do in one-to-one contact.

EDUCATION FOR QUALITY OF LIFE

Comment: I am interested in the quality of relationships as it affects the quality of life. I would especially be interested in comments on the Office of Education's support for school programs dealing with human relations, family relations, and particularly work relations. What emphasis do you give to work as it relates to the community and to interrelations between nations?

Dr. Mattheis: One of the particular areas that we are working on in the Office of Education, as well as in every state, is career education. What we're trying to do is bring about an awareness in the elementary years of what the world of work is all about. The junior high school provides informational material on various occupations and work areas, and high school provides actual experiences, so that when students get out into the world, they can find work in which they are happy, in which they can make a contribution, as they see it, to themselves and to society.

In education, you don't prepare someone for a job in adult life, in industry or on an assembly line, and expect him to accept it as a robot forever. A recent study done by HEW indicated a great deal of dissatisfaction among workers. We do not want to educate people simply to accept what is there. We want to try to give them the basic thought processes and skills so that they can improve what is there.

The single, most rapidly growing area in education is adult and continuing education. Particularly in community colleges and vocational-technical schools, as well as in colleges and universities, adult and continuing education programs have expanded enormously — primarily to provide opportunities and options for individuals we've talked about for a number of years, the people who go into three different occupational areas during a lifetime. Now I think they are moving it up to five or more, by the way. That area of education is an effort to provide increased options for human beings as they move into the middle years and beyond.

THE ROLE OF THE CHURCH

Comment: A student once remarked to the dean of the chapel at Syracuse University: "You know, dean, there is a religious revival going on in America today. It is just a shame that the churches aren't getting in on the action." My question is, what do you see the church doing about the quality of life, or do you see us moving out of the square boxes of the churches to some other form of spiritual expression or study and understanding?

Mr. France: I made a comment earlier about the influence of institutions on people as they develop. It seems to me that each of us is born with certain talents and abilities, and given the nurturing of those, there is no reason why everyone shouldn't be able to reach a level of maturity that ensures a full and happy life. The church ought to be a prime nurturing institution in our society, with respect to the transmission of values and with respect to dealing with problems in an atmosphere that is related to the reality of people's lives.

If the church isn't in on the action, it is because it has not perceived itself as an institution that has the responsibility to provide leadership and direction, to transmit values, and to bring men together to work out their common concerns. The church has to be seen as a key element in this total process of improving the quality of life.

Part One

Cultural and Personal Values

Chapter 1

Western Beliefs and Values and the Quality of American Life

John MacGregor*

This paper is an analysis of five major constellations of related beliefs and values, sometimes called cultural themes, that are predominant in the culture of the Western world and that have important consequences for the quality of life in America. They can be viewed as generating alienation in personal relationships, crisis in our relationship to the environment, and a general deterioration in the quality of life experienced by most members of the society. The net consequence of these cultural orientations has been to generate an overriding concern for standard of living at the expense of quality of life. In this regard, the gross national product seems to be aptly named.

The five cultural themes to be analyzed are the belief system of physicalism and the related value system of materialism, rationalism and the Protestant ethic, objectivism and scientism, social Darwinism and progress, and finally anthropocentrism and active mastery.

PHYSICALISM AND MATERIALISM

The first cultural theme that stands between us and a better quality of life is made up of the belief system of physicalism and the value system of materialism. By physicalism, I mean simply the view that the physical, the concrete, the tangible is the ultimate reality. Physicalism stands in contrast to such orientations as mysticism and idealism. The Yogic belief in the ability of men to move mountains and the Platonic belief in eternal truths that influence the affairs of men are examples of mysticism and idealism respectively. While our physicalism places limitations on our life experiences by narrowing our perceptions of reality, it is the related value system of materialism that generates the more serious problems for our life style. When a society overemphasizes the physical nature of reality, it

*John MacGregor, PhD, is associate professor of sociology and anthropology at Western Washington State College. He obtained his bachelor's degree in sociology with highest honors at the University of Maine and his PhD at Cornell University. As a Fulbright scholar, Dr. MacGregor spent one year of independent field research on postwar social change in a small German farming community.

19

also tends to overvalue material possessions as the visible symbols of the physical world.

Materialism is unquestionably the overriding value system of American society; it predominates in defining institutional arrangements, organizational goals, interpersonal relationships, and of course the stratification system. Our materialism forces us into the merry-go-round of acquisition, conspicuous consumption, waste, planned obsolescence, and more acquisition. This cycle can hardly be viewed as a model for "the good life," but the ecological consequences of such a pattern convert a bad dream into a nightmare. Only in a universe of infinite physical abundance could such an orientation fail to be noxious to life. The vicious cycle of manipulative advertising, impulse buying, increased production, growth of profits, increased pollution, and unsatiated consumer desires is *literally* an insane orientation to reality. Unfortunately, the insanity aggravates, and is aggravated by, the effects of the other cultural themes that guide our lives.

PRAGMATIC RATIONALISM AND PROTESTANT ETHIC

By pragmatic rationalism, I mean simply viewing the world as a set of problems to be solved by rational means. Not all societies look at the world in such terms. Pragmatic rationalism (man over nature) stands in contrast to the views of fatalism (nature over man) and holism (man and nature are one in harmony). Rationalism implies the acquisition of knowledge about how to control nature with such devices and operations as weapons, wheels, irrigation, air conditioning, and hurricane seeding. It implies domination, subjugation, mastery of nature. While many of the fruits of our high standard of living can be traced to rationalism, it is important to realize the price we have paid. One has only to contrast the rape of our land by strip-mining with the Navajo injunction to tread gently on the belly of mother nature — particularly in the springtime when she's pregnant with new life — to get some idea of how much our rationalism has alienated us from nature.

While rationalism is a powerful force on its own, its effects are magnified greatly by a companion value system, the Protestant ethic. As developed in Calvinism, the Protestant ethic enjoins the individual to work hard, to strive, to amass symbols of worldly success, and thereby to prove to himself and to others that he has led a worthy life and has earned the right to a preferred seat in Heaven. Thus, the Protestant ethic is the justification of the worldly activities of rationalist man. It deifies the secular values of the marketplace and the world of work. It makes them not only respectable but divine. Any social costs or consequences — if recognized — are purely secondary to the *accomplishments*. Further, they can be atoned for with acts of philanthropy, which exempt the individual from any blame. The only losers in all of this are the people and resources exploited in the process — a small price to pay in carrying out God's work!

INDIVIDUALISM AND PERSONAL FREEDOM

The third cultural theme which has predominated in the Western framework is made up of the belief of individualism and the value of freedom. By individualism we mean the belief that the individual is more important than the group, that self-interest is the proper goal of all human action.

This doctrine in many ways defines the essence of the Western cultural experience; probably nothing is more central to understanding Western man. While we are justifiably proud of this tradition which attempts to tread the path between authority and anarchy, there are certain alienating consequences which are often ignored although they have been often discussed.

The individual is an ego; he is set off against others who are seen as separate from him. Thus individuals must bridge an unbridgeable gap in order to communicate, cooperate, especially to love. They are essentially alone — and the recognition and acceptance of this fact is one of the primary goals of existential philosophy. The natural relationship of one ego to another is a competitive, striving relationship in the struggle for self-interest. Note how individualism is reinforced by our anthropocentrism (see below).

Individualism can be contrasted with such doctrines as collectivism and communalism. Here the needs of the group take precedence over the individual, who is viewed as simply one representative of the collectivity. It is important to note that the self of collectivism can still be viewed as unique — he does not lose his "individuality" in the act of subordinating his interests to the group. In fact, numerous writers have pointed out that the self of collectivism is more likely to be unique than the ego of individualism, because the removal of ego-ego threat is likely to reduce stereotyping.

The value system of personal freedom extends the alienation of individualism. It tends to emphasize the autonomy of the individual in achieving his own goals and de-emphasize the costs to others in the process. It should be pointed out that the injunction of the youth culture "to do your own thing" implies leaving the other free to do his own thing too, and is much more consistent with collectivism than individualism. Despite much rhetoric and some accomplishments to the contrary, the history of the West can be viewed as a long, painful, alienated process of the privileged few extending personal freedom at the expense of the many. There is a curious consistency to the pattern of freedoms granted which deny the freedom of others, and freedom denied which would benefit only the individual himself. Freedom to kill, freedom to burn, freedom to exploit, freedom to exclude are the freedoms of an individualistic society. Freedom to live, freedom to move, freedom to be are not nearly so well developed. Characteristically, anthropocentric Christianity has supported the process by providing moral justification for the freedoms exercised as well as for the freedoms denied. Thus we have the Crusades, the prayers for victory, the last rites for a condemned killer, the injunctions against abortion, against the sexual freedom of consenting adults, against coffee and tobacco.

The environmental consequences of such an orientation should be obvious. The free Western ego is granted license to exploit the environment in any way that will provide him with personal gain. He can plunder, pillage, rape at will so long as he doesn't violate any of "God's laws". When coupled with anthropocentrism, rationalism, the American frontier spirit and perception of unlimited abundance, the consequences are nothing short of disastrous.

OBJECTIVISM AND SCIENTISM

The fourth cultural theme of concern involves the belief system of objectivism and the value system of scientism. Objectivism is the defining of reality as external to the observer — as "something separate from me." The principal *mode* of objectivism is dichotomization, by which the observer separates reality into mutually exclusive categories, for example, black versus white, false versus true, mind versus body. The initial dichotomy of objectivism is that which separates the observer from the observed. Unfortunately, it is frequently ourselves we are observing; we stand off in a detached way and analyze ourselves, criticize ourselves, compete with ourselves, strive to best ourselves. This is the ultimate in dichotomization and in alienation. It is schizophrenia. Objectivism is in large part responsible for our ability to watch in a curious, detached, bemused way as thousands die in a storm, as men's guts spill on a battlefield or as air pollution makes it more difficult to breath.

The value system that intensifies the effects of objectivism is scientism. Scientism is simply the raising of objective science to the status of a religion. Scientists become the high priests. The astronauts are an extreme example of this. After all, several of them have been 240,000 miles closer to God than the rest of us! Scientism convinces us that our detached approach to reality is responsible for the good life, progress, our standard of living. Where there are problems or failures, science will find the answer. Art, music, poetry, and other intuitive approaches to reality are given little, if any, credence. Even standards of beauty become subsumed under concepts of functionality and pragmatism ("it works — it's *beautiful*"). So, in the technological society our technology generates problems that we believe can only be solved through the application of further technology. At this point the vicious cycle becomes a downhill spiral.

SOCIAL DARWINISM AND PROGRESS

If I am still communicating, you have probably noticed how the various cultural themes we have looked at so far reinforce one another. Western man looks at a material world as a set of problems to be solved in a detached manner by a being who is more out of this world than in it. The detachment of objectivism enables him to ignore problems his own activities have created. The concepts of social Darwinism and progress allow him to delude himself still further with the idea that everything he has created is good.

Social Darwinism is simply the view that Darwinian principles of biological evolution apply to human society as well. Drawing upon the basic concepts of survival of the fittest and natural selection, social Darwinism can be used to justify such arrangements as war, business monopoly, and racism.

Progress is the related value system that defines all change as natural and therefore good. It follows logically, of course, from evolutionary theory itself. If our belief in evolution itself cannot convince us of the rightness of change, the value of progress can provide the necessary delusion. "That's progress," we say, as a bulldozer rips out a forest so that a shopping center can be built. "That's progress," we sigh, as a bulldozer comes across our own land. "That's progress," we gasp as the bulldozer pushes down our home. We have devoted our lives to a rationalistic struggle to achieve, and we *must* be making progress or we would have to view ourselves as failures. To think otherwise would be to know the awful truth of the delusional system we have created. It would be to know that we are locked in a death cycle rather than a life cycle.

ANTHROPOCENTRISM AND ACTIVE MASTERY

I come finally to the combination of the belief system of anthropocentrism and the value system of active mastery. Anthropocentrism is the belief that mankind is the center of the universe, the reason for all being. All societies are anthropocentric to some degree, but I believe that America has developed the idea to the fullest extent. Anthropocentrism is actually the religion of Western society. While we rationalize it by saying that man was made in God's image, the plain fact is that we created God to reflect our egocentric image of ourselves. In doing our duty to the fatherlike image of God, we are actually prostrating ourselves at our own feet. The Bible is the literal storehouse of anthropocentrism. It is full of injunctions to us to have stewardship, to have dominion over the earth and all forms of life upon it. It is the primer for our delusions of grandeur. It reinforces all of the other orientations we have been discussing.

The value system that supports and extends anthropocentrism has emphasized the rightness of man's attempts to exert active mastery over all affairs of the cosmos. It is right that man should tame nature, should subordinate the other species, should conquer space. Man is a *doer*, a *mover*. His manifest destiny is to seize the reigns of control. The most important being in the universe cannot be a passive seer; he must be *on the job*. Thus, a high value is placed on action for action's sake. We scrape away the earth so that we can pour our concrete and erect our steel — so that we can live together in congestion and spend money on artificial parks to replace the natural environment we destroyed in the first place.

We spend billions trying to conquer space, trying to beat other nations to the solution, striving for success despite the expenditure of unimaginable sums of money and the deaths of several astronauts — all of this conveniently blinding us to the press of unresolved problems here on Earth. We strive, compete, "do" when there's nothing to do, feel guilty, bored, or restless when we're on vacation. We assuage the feeling somewhat by taking along our trail bikes, power saws, and water skis. Now our dominion is complete not only on the job, but off the job as well.

THE AUTOMOBILE CULTURE

Let us take a brief look at the "automobile culture" of the United States as a paradigm example of the alienation we are exploring. It is here in this context that the Western cultural themes have reached the point of logical absurdity.

Perhaps the most salient rationalismic struggle of anthropocentric, individualistic Western man is that which centers around overcoming his own perceived inadequacy in the face of such forces as God and Nature. The delusioned system we have been exploring can be seen in the final analysis as an attempt to avoid the admission of man's impotence. Except for the brain, humans are not physically particularly well equipped to fend for themselves in the natural state. Thus a premium has been placed on inventing extensions of man's physiognomy. In a rationalismic, success-oriented society, however, such a process becomes particularly crucial. America's answer has been the automobile.

The automobile is an ideal anthropocentric symbol. It takes relatively puny and defenseless *homo sapiens* and cloaks him in a highly mobile suit of protective armor which can be used as an instrument of death and destruction. In the act of driving, the individual achieves a sense of mastery. Many Americans report that nothing gives them a greater sense of freedom than sliding behind the wheel of the car and roaring down the open road.

The car extends the man in a number of activity and success-oriented ways. It gives him movement, power, status, even sexual potency. It is real, concrete, tangible, physical. It is one of the most important material possessions he can own. The automobile industry is the largest single industry in our economy, and is crucial to our continued concern with material growth, GNP increases, and full employment. While the car virtually becomes part of the man, it also extends objectivism in a number of important ways. The 50,000 highway deaths annually illustrate the degree to which we drive our cars with a "me vs. them" attitude. Similarly, science and technology are of course central to the continued growth and development of the automobile industry. Evolution and progress are similarly central. Evolutionary progress is constantly — nauseatingly — symbolized by the never-ending unveiling of "new" models by the industry. Since there is nothing really new in these models, advertising appeals to our rationalismic-success orientation in order to convince us that the new cars will deliver even more power, more success, more status, more sex. Which once again brings us full circle.

General Motors is perhaps right when it advertises Buick as "something to believe in." *After all, what else is there?*

STEPS TOWARD SOLUTION

The solutions to the problems created by Western man's reality orientation will be neither simple nor easily achieved. The *general directions* such solutions should take, however, are implied by the analysis we have undertaken.

What might be the general outline of such new orientations? First, we desperately need to replace our anthropocentrism with a *life-centered* philosophy which places man in proper perspective among the other species, vis-a-vis ecological balance. Reverence for all life is not wholly foreign to the Western tradition; in fact, we have models like St. Francis and Albert Schweizer to guide us in our attempts. Such an orientation could be merged with a value system more oriented toward *being* rather than *doing*, toward the furtherance of *life* rather than the aggrandizement of the striving individual in his attempts to guarantee personal salvation after *death*. The world-view would reorient us to the knowledge of our precarious existence as a natural species, and would open us up to experiencing the intuitive genius of survival which is the heritage of any evolved species. It would destroy one of the central dichotomies of Western thinking, and with it, hopefully, our tendency to destroy ourselves.

Such a re-orientation would set the stage for all the other desirable steps. Our individualism-freedom theme could hardly thrive in such a context. We would be literally forced to be collectivist, not only among ourselves, but as indicated, in our relation to the rest of the natural world.

Rationalism could be tempered with naturalism, with an attempt to remind ourselves what it is like to live *with* nature. Our hang-up about work, activity, and mastery could be replaced with an ability to "let it be." We need to explore the ways in which we can *truly* return to nature, to decentralize industry, to open up more artisan occupations, to live communally on the land.

Our physicalism would be tempered by all of the above, such that we would see beyond the tangible aspects of life to the intangible aspects beyond. Materialistic concern would give way to concern with quality of life experience, the *meaning* of life in a larger sense. The number of workers currently questioning the "good life" provided by a boring job, a fat paycheck, ever-increasing installment payments, and the amassing of luxury goods is an encouraging sign in this direction. Much of today's youth orientation is similarly encouraging.

Everything we have said indicates the ways in which the new orientation would attempt to eliminate objectivism and dichotomization in our approach to reality. The holistic relationship of organisms and environment becomes the predominant theme. Science and technology are then placed in appropriate perspectives, as aids to the re-defined good life, not as values and ends in themselves. Man is once again in control of his creations.

Finally, our concept of change would replace the idea of growth and development with a sense of process of change that is neither progress nor regress but that simply *is* — in the same sense that life itself simply is. Unceasing and constant, but flowing and moving in waves that go nowhere except on in time. Similarly, value placed on progress could be replaced with a value consistent with the idea of process — it would take the emphasis off of our quest of "onward and upward forever" and free us up to explore a meaningful relationship to the here and now of the present.

If we have been successful in our attempt to conceptualize, we should now have a picture of a fulfilled human in touch with his own sense of the continuity of life, of the right of others to be, satisfied by a rich world of inner experience, integrated with the rest of reality, unimpressed by his own importance, free of the need to strive, to acquire, to worship his own image of himself. This is the man we somehow have to create if we are to overcome the throes of our own death-cycle.

These cultural themes reinforce one another. As an example of this reinforcement, I would point to the way Americans relate to the automobile as a status symbol, as a marvel of technology, as the basis of our materialist economy, as a symbol of active mastery, and as a death machine. Some possible alternatives to these cultural themes can be found, particularly in the youth counterculture. I view our very survival as a society as dependent on the development of more humane values oriented toward persons rather than objects and toward quality of life rather than standard of living.

Chapter 2

Personal Values
in the Middle Years

Seward Hiltner*

I have two statements to make before turning to the central focus of personal values in the middle years of life. For the time being, I ask you to take them — tentatively — for granted.

The first assertion is that the development, cultivation, and exercise of personal values in a fashion appropriate to the heritage of Western civilization cannot be a live possibility for either persons or groups that have not been helped to fulfill basic needs early in their development. The point, for the moment, is that dealing with personal values in the middle years comes out of a history, for good or for ill.

The second preliminary allegation is that personal values in the middle years simply cannot be confined to private or individual concerns, for it is precisely persons in the prime of life upon whom society depends most heavily for cultivating or changing conditions that will make possible the optimal realization of personal values for persons at all other stages of life — infancy, childhood, prepuberty, adolescence, young adulthood, and the older years.

If the personal values of persons in the middle years do nothing positive about values for persons in the other years, then one of three things will happen to a society of this kind. First, it may disintegrate, or "decline," which was Gibbon's word for the fate of the Roman empire. Second, it may actually become, in all of its phases, nothing but a dog-eat-dog aggregation of persons or groups with no real motives but sheer greed and selfishness, however well concealed under honeyed rhetoric, legalistic subterfuge, or prudential evasion and concealment. Third, society might be taken over by an effective revolution of younger persons, despairing that those in the middle years, who are also those with the greatest collective influence, would maintain concern of a proper kind for either their ancestors or their descendants.

*Seward Hiltner, PhD, an outstanding theologian and prolific writer, is professor of theology and personality at Princeton Theological Seminary in Princeton, New Jersey. A recognized leader in pastoral theology, he has been a consultant for the Menninger Foundation in the fields of religion and psychiatry.

I shall return to these two preliminary statements, but I plunge now into my central thesis: that there really is and should be a genuine shift in personal values sometime during the middle years — roughly, between 35 and 50 — and that if the need for this shift remains unrecognized and no shift is made, then the result is the same kind of fixation at this middle stage of life that can occur in the adolescent who confronts adulthood with extreme reluctance, the person of late middle age who denies his entrance into old age, or the beleagured and usually unloved child whose growth becomes arrested at one or another of the stages of childhood development.

CRISIS OF THE MIDDLE YEARS

The truth that there is a genuine crisis of the middle years, regardless of whether a person admits it or not and whether he is successful or not, has of course been foreshadowed in literature. One reason it was only foreshadowed, and not soberly analyzed, was simply that people, on the average, died much earlier than we do today. Until the middle of the nineteenth century, the 50% who survived the first year of life could expect, on the average, to die between 45 and 50. Incidentally, it was much easier to revere aged ancestors when very few of them were around. Today we think of Jesus, who died at 33, as a young man cut off before he could enter the middle years. But in his day, the middle years were probably from 20 or 25 to 35 or 40. Beyond 40, one was in old age.

It is widely recognized today that we have, in the past two or three centuries, greatly extended the time of adolescence. It is just as true, but not so clearly recognized, that we have extended the period of young adulthood, and that the emergence of middle adulthood as different both from early adulthood and old age is a relatively recent phenomenon. To the best of my knowledge, it was the Swiss psychiatrist, Carl G. Jung, who first pointed out that we now confront a genuine crisis in the movement from young to middle adulthood. Jung was analyzing this clearly in the 1920s.

In modern, industrialized societies, Jung believed, no matter how long people go to school or how early they begin to work, the tasks laid before them in young adulthood are — to use a term he invented — extroverted. Men have to get jobs or prepare for better jobs. Whatever their field, and however creative or boring their work, they have to put energy into it. Most of them have to work not just for work's sake but also for the possibility of marriage, of having families of their own. Even those who are celibate from choice or commitment are expected to achieve — even if the nature of their achievements takes such unusual forms as that of the Trappist monk, Thomas Merton.

It is true that Jung's early statements did not foresee all that has happened in the intervening years to women's consciousness, and that he may have thought young adult women to be a kind of brake upon the extroversion of their men. But even disregarding the extreme expressions of the left wing of the women's liberation movement, it seems clear that

Jung's insight about the extroversion of young adulthood would be relevant today about women.

By applying the term extroversion to persons in young adulthood, Jung was not saying that everyone between 21 and 40 was a back-slapping, reflectionless, garrulous person insensitive to the deeper meanings and values of life. He was simply noting the circumstance of this period that in our kind of society has two focuses. First, a person either builds and works ambitiously now, or he enters the middle years with ambiguity and uncertainty. Thus, psychologically, he may not be ready for middle age but may remain fixated forever as a young adult in outlook and values. Second, the period of young adulthood leaves open the possibility of radical changes in life style, type of job, marriage partner, and many other important dimensions. We could add that the feeling characterized by the statement "If I don't like it, I can always change it" is especially strong in our own country with its entire history of pioneering and moving and changing.

But the time comes, whether the person knows it or not, when he either has two cars in the garage or he never will have; when he has a wife, if he is married, with whom he has learned to get along at least tolerably well and at times very well, or he has made a second marriage which is likely to put him, after the second honeymoon, not far from where he was before. He can change companies or cities or adapt his knowledge and skills to advancing science and technology, but the ability he had in young adulthood to make radical shifts has been constantly on the decline. In full middle age, radical shifts are not possible for most people — even though there are always those few creative men and women who can make shifts at any stage of life beyond their teens, like Grandma Moses.

How did Jung understand the crisis (wholly unrecognized by the most people actually going through it) of movement from young to middle adulthood? For him, it was not a crisis over the quantity of psychic energy available. Physical energy might decline bit by bit, as demonstrated by the early retirement of professional athletes. But psychic energy, instead of decreasing, might actually be capable of growing.

If the externals have been handled in tolerable fashion during young adulthood, or if one has during that same period adapted his ambitions to his talents, then he has the potentiality of being less ruled by values of an external nature. He can, if that is so, quite possibly have more psychic energy than he had before, because he can use it more where he wants to than he could before. Even if he has the same job, the same wife, the same children (more nearly ready to leave home of course), the same church, and the same hobby, he can view them from an internal perspective that is more his own. Such a turn might mean merely the emergence of previously concealed or repressed idiosyncrasy — all the way from the extreme privacy-seeking of a Howard Hughes to some innocent, or not so innocent, experiments with sexual interests.

Perhaps Jung's own introversion — another term of his own coinage — made him slant his conception of the crisis. More psychic energy, he believed, should be directed inward, and not just outward, as in the young adult period. For the first time, a man or a woman may begin to get acquainted with those depths of himself or herself which have always been there and have always influenced life and values, but which the external pressures of young adulthood have kept below awareness.

I shall not continue the exposition of Jung's own psychology and how he understood the nature of the depths of the self. On such matters, one might agree with Jung or disagree, but Jung's main point would remain. To put it epigrammatically, this is the time when one either becomes acquainted with deeper levels of his own selfhood, or becomes impoverished through maladaptive concentration on externals. The first shift is not in the content of values, but in where one looks for what is valuable. And for the first time, that look should be more inside than outside.

Today, adherents of acknowledged religions are not alone in their interest in transcendence. Both religious and secular people of many ages recognize that the old way of conceiving transcendence as only outside the self is contradicted by our actual experience — whether that experience be of poets, psychologists, or theologians. Since I am a theologian, perhaps I may be permitted to say that showing transcendence as an inside as well as an outside phenomenon is part of what the Christian teaching concerning the holy spirit is about. Call it what you will, Jung is no longer alone in believing that a deeper look inside reveals something — Jung thought it was individual and universal at the same time — that deepens whatever human-istic values one has and that may produce changes in one's existing values, which, whether good or bad, come more often from outside pushes than from inner choice.

Men, especially, resist this sort of change. Remember that some men in our society are so infused with this cultural virus about toughness that they will not even consult a physician until forced to by extreme pain or persistent relatives. It seems somehow unmanly to shift the focus of vision from the world outside to that within. The more rationalistic a man has proved to be in his young adulthood — whether he be a physicist or a plumber — the harder it is for him not only to make such a shift but even to examine the evidence that would suggest, for example, that it is just as important in middle age as it was in his late teens or twenties to learn a profession, trade, or type of work. The special difficulty encountered by men does not mean that women, libbers or otherwise, make the transition easily. If only there were some clear and observable change that could not be overlooked by the self and others — such as is evident in the emergence of puberty, or in the gradual physical decline of the older years — then the middle-aged person would have to admit that he should at least take a new look. But there is no such outward sign. What, then, tends to happen at this stage of life?

It is no accident, I believe, that the period of transition between young and middle adulthood — roughly the ages between 35 and 45 —

is marked for a large number of people not by the desirable confrontation of the self in a new way and at new depths, as advocated by Jung, but rather by deleterious habits and behavior patterns, not a few of which come to the attention of physicians. Although this is not the peak period when people die from diseases with clear psychological elements, it is the period when such diseases get firm root and then persist unless there can be successful intervention. Divorce rates are high for people in this age range, and perhaps even more common than divorce — especially among professional people, as some recent studies suggest — are tacit recontracts of marriage, which keep intimacy to a minimum. This is also the period when people become more one-sided.

It is the rare person, couple, or group that is not tempted to use what Karl Menninger has called coping devices to avoid even admitting that a crisis is present, despite the absence of external signs. Whatever the devices used (they may or may not be harmful in themselves), the net effect is a continuing blindness about what is necessary to confront what Jung called "the second half of life" and to find and exercise the values peculiarly suited for it. If education can help people make shifts and take new and deeper looks inside — even at times by means that are somewhat less than the best, if necessary — then the crisis can be confronted and the values reaffirmed or changed as exploration suggests.

WHAT CAN WE DO?

Clearly, the first thing to do is to try education, however informal it may be or whatever the context — the medical office, the pastor's study, the personnel department, or perhaps even the communications media. The essential thing at this stage of life is self-exploration, with the aim of finding value in solitude and more meaning in human relationships. Those of us who are trained in one way or another to be special helpers to our fellow human beings can encourage this enterprise. Every time we are called upon to assist a person with a problem relevant to our special fields, we can ask ourselves a question, if the person is in the latter stages of young adulthood or has already entered middle adulthood: Aside from the individuality of the problem, to what extent is it a concealed and unhelpful coping device to prevent confrontation with the crisis that middle adulthood brings?

I recently had a short series of pastoral counseling sessions with a married couple in their 40s. The husband had been conducting an eat-his-cake-and-have-it-too life for some years, while his wife, always believing, falsely, that he would come around if only she loved him enough and showed it, had closed her eyes and lived a doormat existence. Her eyes were opened by genuine but short-lived interest from another man, and she determined not to go on as things were. She proposed divorce, but at that point her husband returned, gave up his girl friends, and came to me expecting that I would support his desire to reinstate the *status quo ante*. The wife rather expected to be lectured on the evils of separation or divorce, but she was confused enough to want any enlightenment that could be provided.

As our conversations proceeded, it became clear that the husband was prepared to change his behavior, at least for the time being, but was not ready even to examine his underlying attitude. To him, the only problem was persuading his wife and me that he had reformed. On her side, the wife began to see that she had been exploited, first as doormat for several years and then as a romantic in danger of reading virtues into men who only listened to her and treated her romantically.

I gave no advice, but the wife did insist on a temporary separation. The husband acquiesced instead of filing a nasty countersuit, as he had threatened to do. Whether there is a chance of their coming together again in a changed relationship remains to be seen, but it is unlikely. The wife gained more from these sessions, in my judgment, because I think she is now critical of her romanticism. The husband, I fear, is as unready for self-exploration as he was when they first consulted me. As with everybody, their problems had individual dimensions, but I saw throughout the different ways both of them used to avoid confronting the crisis of middle years.

At this point I can hear very busy people — not only physicians but also my brother clergymen — asking how in the world time can be found to do the kind of thing I have just illustrated. It may be that many doctors and clergymen literally have neither the time nor the skill, but I believe there are two factors that render this line of argument null. The first is that more and more people in various professions are being trained for short-term assistance in the middle-years crisis, but they may never get a crack at the patient or the parishioner unless the doctor or the clergyman offers a suggestion, with reasons. The other factor is that a brief explanation may help a lot of intelligent and emotionally healthy people. Merely hearing briefly from some authoritative person like a physician or a clergyman that their peculiar problem may be partly cultural — in the sense that they are entering or passing through a crisis that our society generally does not even recognize as such — may be enough to help them confront it. I can recall a wise doctor, not a psychiatrist, who gave me such a word while I was in my 30s. It took about five extra minutes of his time, but it greatly affected what I did about it from then on.

BEFORE AND AFTER THE MIDDLE YEARS

Returning to the preliminary points made at the start of this discussion, I can now strengthen them. First, it was declared that what is done to help persons at previous stages of development is inseparably related to the ability to confront the middle-years crisis, with its great opportunity and its possible tragedy. Here is where therapy, treatment, education, re-education, and rehabilitation need to look ahead toward the coming crisis of entrance into the middle years. If, by our work, we help only with immediate problems (which we must of course do) with no sense that even a partial understanding or solution is a gain for all of life and with no sense that the courage to look beneath the immediate problem is an asset at any age, then we are off the track. As I have tried to show, the problems of many people require very little additional time on our part, and when more time is needed, let us get over our snootiness about legalistic standards for helpers. Fortunately, more helpers with better training are available all the time. In my own profession there are, of course, great variations in degrees of understanding, training, and skill, but at no time in human history have so many clergymen had as much ability to provide such help as now. In recent workshops with clergymen in Texas, Georgia, and New Jersey, I found no difference at all in basic understanding and skill in these matters.

At the beginning, I alleged also that the consideration, or reconsideration, of personal values that is called for by the crisis of the middle years must recognize the influence of people in this age range on the conditions for growth, development, and enrichment in the lives of persons at all other ages. For example, we may not be experts on either nursery schools or nursing homes, but we should be sufficiently concerned, as a result of our head-on confrontation with the middle-years crisis, that proper standards and programs are in effect and that qualified people are in charge of both enterprises. If one has taken a long look at the crisis in his own middle years, and has made some constructive alterations in the inwardness and spontaneity with which he conceives his personal values, then he will be immediately aware that our society is ambivalent toward teen-agers and older people. Toward children, our conscious attitude is a bit better; we do try harder. But our effort may still be hampered by the remnants of thinking that children will make it only if they become like us. Consciously, we reject that old chestnut, but it still seems pervasive to me as an unconscious attitude. It may play a part in what needs to be changed about our educational system, which is controlled by those in the middle years.

I do not believe any of our basic institutions — including medicine, education, and the church — are operating near their potential capacity to enhance personal values, which are the sole base upon which genuine social values can be built. But we are not bankrupt in any of these areas. The family is not going to be old hat in 1980. Pray God the church will change some of its programs, but in the direction of integrating personal and social values under the equal influence of religion and common sense. Some aspects of health-care delivery are bound to be changed, for too many people do not receive even the basic services.

Some of you may wonder why I have made no reference to some of the rapidly changing personal values in our society — why I have not roundly condemned moral standards that say anything goes. Without denying that I am concerned and even alarmed by hard drugs, the abundance of violence, the continuing discrimination against minority groups, and even the tendency of the young to follow the peer group and ignore the parents and other adults in forming their personal values, I can only answer that even though there are novel features in all of these phenomena, none of them is wholly new, and an extraordinary number of the worst of them are really imitations of their elders.

In a heterogenous society, no personal values can ever take root — in the sense that they become intrinsic — if the adult guides and guarantors simply seek conformity in behavior. Personal values mean responsibility — responsibility not as a burden, but as a road to fulfillment. In this form, they are also the social values our society needs.

Chapter 3

The Roles We Play

Bernice L. Neugarten*

Middle age, whether you think it ranges from 25 to 65 or from 40 to 50, is a many-faceted thing. It is not all boredom and worry about losing your job, about the menopause, or about retirement. As a matter of fact, the middle years are no different from other periods of life in that they have their goods and their bads, their ups and their downs. There are some good things about being 25, and 40, and 60, and 80.

Our society still puts a lot of faith in stereotypes that, for the most part, are not true. Let's examine menopause in the middle-aged woman. There are many myths about menopause based on the experiences of those few women who take their problems to specialists — physicians, psychiatrists, social workers, or psychologists. The average woman is generally happy, not unhappy, over the menopause. That statement is based on my experience in talking with and studying a great many women. They are glad to be free of the menstrual cycle and the worry of pregnancy. They are generally aware that the menopause may bring discomfort, but they are also fully aware that they are going to live through it. They take it pretty much in stride.

We found that only two out of a hundred women even mention the menopause as a major problem of middle age. Or to put it differently, if you go out into the community and ask hundreds of women what worries them, the menopause will seldom be mentioned. Yes, women would like to know more about it — they haven't had very much information — but they see more good things about it than bad.

Feelings about retirement is another example of stereotyping. Many good studies based on national samples show that men, as they actually approach retirement, are less desirous of retiring than they were five years before. It is also true that a lot of men go through a stressful period of readjustment after they retire, which may last between six months and a year. But most men learn to use their time in ways they like, and it is more and more true that men choose to retire as soon as they have enough money

---

*Bernice L. Neugarten, PhD, is professor and chairman of the Committee on Human Development at the University of Chicago and past president of the Gerontological Society. In 1971 she was named winner of the Kleemeier Award by the Gerontological Society for her outstanding contributions to research in aging.

36

to live at a level they think is comfortable. As you know, the retirement age is dropping. A larger proportion of people today are retiring at 60 and 55. Work is terribly boring for most people in this society, and they give it up with more pleasure than displeasure.

Society is changing. It no longer operates on the principle that a person's worth is measured by his work. More and more of us are taking our pleasure from leisure rather than from work. In some aspects our society has turned upside down. A hundred years ago, the higher one's education and income, the more leisure one had. Now, a small proportion of the best educated and the most skilled professionals and business executives are the people who put in 60- and 80-hour weeks. As you go down the occupational scale, people are working fewer hours. They are working 40- and 37½- and then 35-hour weeks. It is the blue-collar worker who has gained leisure over the past 100 years. But top-level business executives, the career-driven people, are working harder than ever.

THE LIFE CYCLE

I'm not accustomed to thinking of the total span from 25 to 65 as the middle years. I think that range is too great. Go out and ask people how they would divide the life cycle after a person is about 21. If you interview hundreds of people at length, what usually emerges is a view that adulthood is divided into at least four stages. There is a period that most people call youth, a period that most people call maturity, a period that most people call middle age, and then a period that most people call old age.

The ages people assign to these periods of adulthood vary according to occupational status. To a blue-collar worker or to someone who has only been employed off and on throughout his life, aging seems to happen very rapidly. Youth is short, maturity and middle age are short, and old age begins early. The average blue-collar worker will tell you that a man is old at 60. For him, middle age begins at 35. A lawyer or a physician or a dentist or a business executive, male or female, views the life cycle as stretched out by comparison. For professionals and white-collar workers, there is a long period of youth when people grope around for the right job and try out the world in various ways. Then there is another long period of getting established and then an enormously long middle age. They feel that a man is not old until he is 70 or 75.

Historically, middle age and adolescence are 20th century social inventions. At one time, children moved immediately from childhood to adulthood. They began work at age 7 or 8 or 10, and they went from a short life as a child to a long adult work life and an early death. With the invention of adolescence, we had the stretching out of childhood. Now we have a new invention called youth. Some people talk about youth as a period in which young people, and particularly affluent young people, try to decide where they fit into society. It is not adolescence really and it is not adulthood. It is yet another period.

THE MIDDLE YEARS

There are advantages to life at every age. Very few middle-aged people want to be young again. They want to feel young. They want to maintain their youthful attitudes. But they wouldn't trade their present position at 40 or 50 to be 20 or 25 again. Is the proportion of people who are unhappy at 50 any greater than the proportion who are unhappy at 20? We don't know, but no age group in this society has a monopoly on alienation, boredom, unhappiness or dissatisfaction with the establishment, the rat race, or anything else.

I know many people, and so do you, who at 40 and 50 feel that they are in their prime. They feel that it has taken them 20 years to attain their expertise, and they now know how to deal with their lives. They are more mellow, more able to take what life brings. These are the people, in all levels of our society, who will tell you that life at 40 and 50 turned out to be better than they expected. And this is a side of adulthood that has not come to the attention of the mass media and society. There have not been enough attempts to break down the stereotypes that we live with about middle age and old age.

People in their 40s and 50s are a group in which I have had some special interest. In this group one finds some very interesting gratifications as well as some interesting new developments. This tends to be the period when people have a reversal in their time perspectives. They begin to reckon time backward from death rather than forward from birth. To put it another way, they begin to think of how much time there is left, not how much time they have lived. So they start thinking about what things they still want to do. Many people at this age say they now have time to do the things they wanted to do before, and they are going to do them.

There are enormous differences between men and women in the way they approach middle age. This is a period when women are likely to tell you that they have new freedom. Middle-aged women in this society feel that they have two lives to live. One is over by age 40. They have devoted their time to raising children, if they haven't been in the work force as well, and they can look forward to another 30 to 40 years. They can start all over again. Some of them go back to school, more than half go back to work. So the typical young child in our society now sees his grandmother at work and his mother at home.

Women will talk about their freedom, but men don't — at least not the men we have studied. Men seem to think of life as one cycle that begins to turn downward at about 45 or 50. They are the ones, for the right reasons, who are worried about their health. They are worried about the heart attack. They are worried that they can no longer count on their bodies. Women don't worry about their health. They don't worry excessively about the menopause, as I have already said. They worry about their husbands' health, and they rehearse for widowhood.

Just as the major problem of middle-aged women is not the menopause, it is also not the empty nest. Most women are glad to see their children grow up, leave home, marry, and have their careers. The notion that they mourn the loss of their reproductive ability and their mother-role does not seem to fit modern reality. No matter what the stereotypes tell us, it is not the way women talk when you listen.

CHANGING RHYTHMS

The society in which we live is changing so rapidly that it is changing the rhythm of the whole life cycle. Not only do we have ever-greater longevity, but events in the life cycle are also at a different pace. Until the last year or two, the marriage age was dropping steadily. Women and men were marrying younger and having their first child within the first year of marriage. Thus, the family cycle is developing a different rhythm. Then there is this long, long period of middle age and old age to which people can look forward. And look forward they do! The image of old age is no longer that of the old person in a rocking chair; it is the old person on the golf course. The fact that more and more of us are going to live longer raises many questions about effects on society.

Discussion

PANELISTS

Bernice B. Neugarten, PhD, professor and chairman of the Committee on Human Development at the University of Chicago.

John MacGregor, PhD, associate professor of sociology and anthropology at Western Washington State College.

ALIENATION AND AGISM

Dr. Neugarten: It has almost become a fad today to consider yourself alienated. Actually, most people aren't very alienated from society because they are achievement-oriented, which means they internalize the values of society.

Six cultural values — materialism, pragmatic rationalism, scientism, social Darwinism, individualism, and anthropocentrism — have often been used to characterize American society. These are values that perhaps are going to be hard to maintain in an aging society. Ten percent of our population is now 65 and over. It is not unlikely that in 20 years, 16% of the population will be over 65. If that happens it is going to be hard to maintain a pragmatic, do-it-yourself, nonreflective society. Maybe that should give us hope.

Dr. MacGregor: I see two possibilities: The aging of our society may be a tremendous stimulant for the development of new value orientations, or it may result in a clash between our aging population and our outmoded value system. We may have increased numbers of people who don't know how to use their leisure time and who are frustrated by the conditions of retirement.

Dr. Neugarten: I agree. One phenomenon of this society is agism — a negative attitude toward age groups other than one's own. And agism, like racism and sexism today, might come to characterize this society in the future. We may be facing a situation in which the antagonism between age groups is growing, although the situation is very ambivalent and a countertrend is also visible. Agism characterizes our attitudes toward the young. But, if this attitude works downward, it also works upward, with negative attitudes toward the old. So the question is whether we can look forward to greater divisiveness between age groups or greater cohesion in the next couple of decades.

Dr. MacGregor: I indicated earlier that most Americans internalize the values of their society. Dr. Neugarten made a point that I would like to underscore. If you are living in a society that has alienating values, then it is a creative act if you separate yourself from that society and make a positive decision to attempt to change it in a constructive way. In other words, to participate in an alienated society is to expose yourself to alienation from self, alienation from others, and alienation from nature. To refuse to participate in society's alienating ways is to move toward exploring ways to reduce alienation.

ALTERNATIVE WORLD VIEWS

Comment: What are the alternatives to the world view and value pairs that Dr. MacGregor cited? Many people make similar criticisms that are scarier after dark, as far as I'm concerned.

For example, what are the alternatives to his five pairs? Are they spiritualism and immaterialism, irrationalism and mysticism, subjectivism and antisocial regression, and subservience, deicentrism, and abject despair? Although my question may seem contentious, it is really impossible for a Jewish psychoanalyst wearing a MacGregor plaid to be an antagonist to a Scotch sociologist wearing an Old Testament beard.

Dr. MacGregor: I feel that there is a desperate need to raise the critical issues and simply get people to question what we are doing now. But it is also important to ask where we go from here.

I have been inspired by the counterculture, that is, the serious efforts of a core group of young people to explore a value system that stands in contrast to the present one. I don't think it is a matter of simple dualistic contrast. Really, young people are asking us to go back and explore certain values that somehow got lost in the shuffle. As a matter of fact, most of our value orientations are variations along continuums. Our man-over-nature concept is one extreme, the fatalistic acceptance of nature over man is the other, and the holistic view of man in harmony with nature is somewhere in between. So my answer is that we don't need new values, but reemphasis, or movement along a continuum.

It is crucial to me as a sociologist to recognize how distorted our values have become through the process of industrialization and bureaucratization. Big industry, mass production, the organization-man syndrome — these relatively recent developments in American society have latched onto certain values in our total value tradition and utilized them for the purposes of building our vast industrialized economic structure. But those values have served their purpose. They have helped create the high standard of living that we like to flaunt, but it is time to reemphasize certain other values.

Dr. Neugarten: Maybe I'm taking the position of empiricist or skeptic, but when we talk about changing the society, we really ought to be talking about who gains and who loses. What is the evidence that in other times a higher proportion of the people were better off? I'm not saying that we have the best society or that everything is rosy, but we should be a little more searching in these questions. Who is to decide what the quality of life should be? And for whom? Sometimes we are very sure that one set of values is better than another, but aren't we really comparing extremes when we make judgments like that?

Dr. MacGregor: I'm not concerned about when and if things were better. I'm concerned about whether we can develop value yardsticks. The challenge is to see if society can be better than it is now.

Dr. Neugarten: If you are saying that what we need are some good social indicators instead of just economic indicators, I'm on your side.

Comment: What are those values that are bad which the counterculture is correcting?

Dr. MacGregor: The counterculture represents a turning away from the prevalent value orientations to some degree — an orientation toward a whole new set of values: independence, social responsibility, spontaneity, sharing, and honesty. I mean by the counterculture, however, a relatively small group of people seriously committed to exploring more humane values. Most of these people are now in rural communes in the hills someplace. These people have a serious commitment to exploring more humane life styles. Many of them are associated with what has come to be called the Jesus movement. I think they represent an alternative to the traditional value system. I think it is tragic that many of us are threatened by the development and that we write it off as just another form of juvenile delinquency or attach some similar stereotype to it.

Comment: I won't go the counterculture route to conquer alienation, so my question is how would you move from alienation? If you want to replace economic values with more humane values, how do you describe that transition?

Dr. Neugarten: We seem to be oversimplifying the world and people terribly. I haven't known very many members of the counterculture who didn't have strong drives toward comfort. The number of kids living in communes, I think, is a tiny number, and I would guess that the average life of those groups is under two years. Nor do I think that the young have a monopoly on the values you speak of. There are great numbers of middle-aged and old people who have spoken out throughout the history of American society for the same humanistic values. It is a fact that the mass media frequently talk about trends as if they were new.

The whole thing is much more complex than we have implied in our discussion, and there is really no way of grasping that complexity. Every one of us is a mixed bag. We exhibit all of these values, good and bad. Today you beat the bus driver out of a fare, but next spring you don't cheat on your income tax. That is the complexity of life.

Comment: I wonder whether much of the solution to the problem we are discussing lies in an attempt to restore a sense of community. Much of the success that we have had so far in improving the quality of life evolves from strategies directed not so much at delivering an individual service but building in the community supports to go along with it — the institutional services and community leadership. I wonder if communes are not really an attempt to find a sense of community geographically and ideologically.

Dr. MacGregor: When you talk about decreasing levels of alienation in this society, you are partly and clearly talking about restoring certain kinds of community spirit and community relatedness that have been lost. You are asking the broader question of how we can get away from our one-sided value commitments. That is the whole challenge for us to explore over the next few years. One concept that characterizes this challenge happens to go back to our religious tradition.

I'm certain that Dr. Hiltner would concur that we are talking about a concept of transcendence. We are talking about transcending our present extrasensual selves to become richer, more open, broader personalities, and I think we are going to need a lot of community support to do that. Another hopeful phenomenon is the whole growth psychology movement to which Hugh Downs alluded. We need group support for our efforts to become more humane with one another — and not necessarily groups as extreme as those represented by the counterculture.

Comment: I admire the ingenuity with which Dr. MacGregor made his distinction between cultural values, but we make a big mistake in trying to cut them apart. Some of the confusion in what we have heard today comes from our failure to realize that. Actually, they all boil down to variations on the same theme: the maintenance of an individualistic ego by physical control over the environment. For example, the only reason we can talk about anthropocentrism is that our objective scientism led us to the knowledge of it.

ROLES AND PERSONAL RELATIONSHIPS

Comment: In our society we lump many conflicting roles into the early part of the middle years. I wonder if there are societies that have successfully spread these roles out through the later years in life.

Dr. Neugarten: If we really wanted to change the value system, one of the pragmatic things we could do is exactly what you are suggesting but not saying — that is to mix education, leisure, and work so they are not age-graded. We keep education for the young, we keep work for the middle-aged, and we keep leisure for the old. If we can get a better mix of those things, we'll have more freedom in society. We are beginning to see middle-aged and old people going to school — and not just for vocational gain — so we can hope to see this kind of mix in the next couple of decades.

In our society, the role load in these years is heavier for the female than for the male. Young women come to maturity in a synchronistic way; that is, around 20 or 25 they take on marriage, a family, and possibly a work role as well. But for males the trend has been to stay longer and longer in school so that economic maturity does not occur at the same time as family maturity does. I presume that as more of us live longer and raise our children younger, more women will take a seriate approach to their roles. They will do some things now and delay others, doing them one after another rather than piling them up.

Comment: Dr. Hiltner made reference to the divorce rate during the middle years, and I think the implication was that the high rate of divorce is the result of the confusion created by the crisis of the middle years. I wonder if it might not, instead, be the result of the clarity that the crisis of middle age creates — by that I mean the increased perception and awareness of personal values that can result from the self-analysis that is characteristic of the middle years.

Dr. Neugarten: You know, the reverse of that question has often struck me; that is, I often wonder how it happens that people stay together after 20, 30, and 40 years. We know that the longer people live, the more different from other people they become. There must be something about marriage that acts like a rubber band — stretching with time. Traditionally, the differentiation has proceeded more rapidly in the male of a couple, but I think in the last ten years, it is happening just as rapidly with women. So, I for one am not all that impressed with the rise in the divorce rate in middle years. If there is a bulge in the divorce rate of the middle-aged, it is not a very major bulge. Evidently most people find some greater good in staying together than in breaking up, and I presume that the duration of the relationship has an effect here. I imagine that a couple builds and shares experience over the years and that must enrich a relationship.

Comment: Being single and 30 in today's world where more young people are staying away from marriage, I wonder if you have any comments or statistics on how single persons relate to the aging process.

Dr. Neugarten: At present, the aging single person has by far the worse situation. Most of the measures that we have of life's satisfactions, such as contentment and physical and mental health, are in favor of the married. Also, most married people have children. Something like 80% of old people in the United States have children, and of that high proportion, about 80% see at least one child once a week. This is in contradiction to the stereotype in our society that we isolate and dump old people. We don't. The family doesn't dump its old.

Dr. MacGregor: Relatively speaking, it dumps more than it should. Again, my concern is not how we compare with other societies or other times. But we can say that there is an ideal in terms of integrating old people with the younger generations of the family, and we can ask where we fall short of the ideal.

Dr. Neugarten: It happens that most of the old people in the United States today don't want to live with their children. You can say they should want to, but they actually don't.

Parenthood

Chapter 4

Parenting — The Hope of the Future

Lee Salk*

The concept of quality of life is something that has been written about by other people in the recent past. I'd like to quote from a book written by Van Rensselaer Potter, *Bioethics: Bridge to the Future*, published in 1971. Dr. Potter made the following statement: "Mankind is urgently in need of new wisdom that will provide the 'knowledge of how to use knowledge' for man's survival and for improvement in the quality of life." This concept of wisdom as a guide for action, the knowledge of how to use knowledge for the social good, might be called the "science of survival," surely, the prerequisite to improvement in the quality of life. Dr. Potter says, "I take the position that the science of survival must be built on the science of biology and enlarged beyond the traditional boundaries to include the most essential elements of the social sciences and the humanities with emphasis on philosophy in the strict sense, meaning 'love of wisdom'." I think that what Dr. Potter wrote encompasses everything with which we are concerned here.

As many of you know, I have been working in my career many years, trying to help people with emotional disorders. I have spent a tremendous amount of time working with relatively few people and have achieved relative success, but it is relatively little success in terms of what we could achieve if we focused on the problems of prevention.

Mental health statistics are absolutely astounding. At this very moment, 50% or more of all hospital beds in this country are occupied by people suffering from some serious emotional disorder. The average length of stay is tremendously long. If every physician, every psychologist, every social worker, every nurse, every paraprofessional were put to the task of treating these people for their emotional disturbances, we couldn't even begin to solve the problem. For this reason, I think we have to start looking more towards the prevention of these problems.

I think that most people realize that these problems have their roots in early infancy and childhood experiences, the environmental conditions under which people are born and grow. We must begin to focus our at-

*Lee Salk, PhD, is clinical professor of psychology in pediatrics at Cornell University Medical College and director of the Division of Pediatric Psychology for the New York Hospital-Cornell Medical Center.

tention not only on educating parents, but also on educating professionals to the importance of parenthood. From day to day, parents are confronted with problems in raising their children, and they actually have no one to turn to for help with these kinds of problems. They usually call an aunt, an uncle, a mother-in-law, or a neighbor, and they get all sorts of information that has no basis in scientific fact. Parents are highly receptive to all kinds of information, true or not, if they feel that what is offered will help them help their children. Actually, they are the most neglected people in our population. The pediatrician is in the position of being the person to offer this kind of information, but most people realize that the pediatrician is extremely busy and does not have the time to spend with the parent who has a normal, emotional problem. Unfortunately, normal emotional problems that are not handled correctly turn out to be serious emotional problems, and then they require psychiatric help.

We have to do something about educating people in parenthood. I consider parenthood the most important role any human being can assume in life. And yet it is the one role for which we have the least amount of preparation. I would say more people spend more time finding an authorized mechanic for their car than they do finding a qualified person to take care of their child.

ANIMAL RESEARCH AND HUMAN BEHAVIOR

A lot of information we have acquired in the field of psychology about human behavioral development comes from animal experiments. A number of my colleagues in the field of psychology study rats, for example. When we psychologists who study the human being began to look upon their data and wonder if the same phenomena occur in human behavior, most of them tended to look down upon us. Recently, however, when I found that a number of my colleagues were encouraging us to go on with our studies of human development, I became rather suspicious. I asked one of them, and he said, quite confidentially, we are really still interested in under-standing the rat better, and we consider the human being a good model for the study of rats.

There is always a danger in generalizing from animal experiments or animal behavior to human behavior, but it is equally dangerous to avoid some of the findings we acquire in animal experimentation that may have bearing on the human. So, while we can't jump that fence very easily, I think we should develop hypotheses that are built on animal research.

Environmental Influences on Behavioral Development

Let me tell you a little bit about some of the experiments that have been done to show that early experiences have a tremendous impact on later behavior. In this Congress, we are talking about the middle years, but what happens in the middle years depends to a great extent upon what happened in the early hours, days, weeks, months, years of life.

In the middle 30s, Dr. David Levy did some rather fascinating experiments with chicks and with puppies. He took some chicks that had just hatched and put them in an apparatus that prevented them from pecking on the ground in the normal fashion. Their food was in a trough, and they had to peck forward to get the grain. He kept them in this apparatus for a given period of time in their very early development. Some weeks later, he removed them from the apparatus and put them in a perfectly normal environment with the grain and food spread on the ground. He found that these chicks would peck at the grain, but would never seem to get it. They would see the grain and peck at it, but they would constantly miss it. And there was nothing that could be done that would help undo this problem. It seems these chicks required certain environmental conditions during this period of neurological development to develop what seemed to be an adaptive response that would enhance survival. When environmental conditions interfered with the development of this response, the animal lost forever its capacity to eat normally. This exemplifies the point that what a biological organism needs at a given stage in its development cannot be made up for later on.

Dr. Levy did some other studies with dogs. He took puppies away from their mothers long before they were ready to be weaned, and found that, as they went through dog adolescence and adulthood, they were terribly destructive. They would bite the legs of tables and chairs and chew them to bits. They would rip bedspreads off of beds. There was no aversive condition that he could provide that would in any way alter this destructive behavior.

Many people in the behavioral sciences have used these data to support the thesis that oral frustrations can lead to oral aggressiveness. You can look upon it that way, or you can look upon it as simply learning. If an organism is deprived of what it needs during a period of its life, it is preoccupied throughout its life with gratification of that need. If you want an infantile need to go away, satisfy it and it goes away. Strangely enough, in our culture we think that we should not satisfy people. We believe that if they are satisfied, they are just going to want to be satisfied all the time. Actually, we have various kinds of hunger that need to be gratified so that we can get on to the next developmental stage. I often tell the parents I teach that this is like the attitude of not satisfying your infant because, if you do, that baby is going to want to be a baby all of its life. Actually, the opposite is true. If you satisfy the needs, they go away; the child is then free to take on the next task in his development. It is like saying to someone, "Don't have lunch when you get hungry, because you might enjoy your lunch so much that you eat and eat and eat until you just burst." That is obviously ridiculous.

We know that people who are hungry and who are not given satisfaction with food become preoccupied with food. In studies done by Dr. Murray at Harvard many years ago they deprived students of food for many hours. After a period of time, the students were given pictures to look at, and were asked to make up stories with a beginning, a middle, and an end. Dr. Murray found that most of the stories concerned food, hunger, and oral frustration. It meant that the students tended to perceive the world in terms of their unmet needs. A control group of students was given the same pictures to look at, and they perceived other aspects of reality. This tells you that hungry people see the world in terms of their hunger, and that children who are frustrated will see the world in terms of their frustrations.

There was another study done at the University of Toronto about 15 years ago by a man named Weininger. He was experimenting with rats, teaching them to run a maze in a given way. Half the animals were being used for experimental purposes, and the other half were being used for control purposes. The control animals were not being held or touched during this phase of the experiment. One night, the temperature apparatus in the laboratory broke, and when Weininger came into his laboratory the next day, he found that half the animals were alive and the other half were dead. The living ones were the ones that had been run through the mazes. The ones that had died were the control animals, the ones that had not been touched. In true scientific fashion, he repeated the experiment and found essentially the same thing. This opened a whole new area of investigation in the field of experimental psychology called "handling." Psychologists began to look at all the parameters of early handling, and they found that if young animals were handled a great deal during their early development, they seemed to be able to withstand more stress later in life. They showed more exploratory behavior, fewer aversive reactions to members of their own species, etc.

When psychologists began to study the physiological aspects of handling behavior, they found it affected the adrenal glands in the adrenal-pituitary axis. They were able to see that certain environmental conditions during early development caused a structural change within the body and that this structural change seemed to persist into the animal's adulthood, giving the animal a greater capacity to deal with stress later on. What I'm trying to point out is that environmental conditions during a critical stage in development can affect the structure of the organism so that it makes a more adaptive response at the psychological level. In other words, there is an interplay between the environment, the mind, and the body.

Sensory Deprivation

Another series of rather fascinating experiments was done by Dr. Hebb at McGill University. He wanted to see the effect of early sensory deprivation on the behavior of dogs. At random, he divided litters of Scottish Terriers into experimental and control groups. The experimental animals were isolated in cages where they saw no members of their own species or any human beings. They were fed through a double-doored compartment, and their cages were cleaned in such a way that they did not see anyone for a given period of time. This period of isolation began immediately after the animals were weaned. The control animals were farmed out to professors at McGill University which, for some reason, was thought to be a normal environment. In any event, it was a more stimulating environment.

At the conclusion of the experimental stage, these animals were brought together to see what effects environment had had on their behavior. The results were rather astounding. When the experimental animals were taken out of their cages and allowed into a room that had a painted grid on the floor so the experimenter could measure the activity of the animals in a given period of time, these animals would just come out and stand there. Many of them would spin around and twirl. They would never look at the experimenter; they showed no exploratory behavior; and when the experimenter shocked them with a cattle-prodder, they would yelp, jump up, and come down again, but they wouldn't walk away, even when shocked repeatedly. In comparison, those raised in the homes of McGill professors, upon entering the experimental room, immediately ran all over the place, wagging their tails, sniffing in every corner, and darting back and forth until they became familiar with the environment. When the experimenter came by with the cattle-prodder and poked them once, shocking them, the animals yelped, ran away, and would not go near the experimenter again. These dogs were able to learn on the basis of one trial. In the follow-up on these animals, it seemed that this behavior persisted well into their adulthood.

If any of you has seen autistic children, you would be singularly impressed by how similar these control animals were in behavior to autistic children. But again, I hasten to add that we cannot draw a one-to-one analogy between humans and animals.

PREVENTION OF DISTURBED BEHAVIOR

The thing that has amazed me over the years is the fact that all behavioral scientists, no matter what field they come from, no matter what their experiences, whether they be psychoanalysts, behavior modification psychologists, or what have you, all recognize the importance of early experience on later behavior, but for some reason they do not want to contaminate themselves by studying it. This body of knowledge about the effects of early experience on later behavior is in the psychological literature, but it does not seem to get from there to the consumer, meaning the parent, the pediatrician, the other people on the front line in mental health who ought to take this knowledge and apply it in the prevention of disturbed behavior.

In our institution a number of years ago we recognized that mothers had questions they wanted to ask of a pediatrician, and we felt we ought to give them some opportunity to meet and talk with one. So, they relegated this task to the most junior intern we had on the staff. He not only did not like doing it, but also considered it one of those jobs that came with being the lowest man on the totem pole. The other thing about it that I think is rather astounding is he had no training for answering these questions in the first place, which made it a very dangerous situation.

Parenting

This kind of attitude has persisted over the years; we don't want to discuss parenthood. Parenthood is something that just comes naturally, or is relatively unimportant, and we assume that everyone knows what they have to do. Because of this attitude, parents have been confused and bombarded with all sorts of conflicting information. Some people will tell you to pick up your baby when it cries, but most people will tell you that that will spoil it, that you should let it cry. You get some people who will say that your baby can see when it is born, but many more will say that it can't see anything until it is six weeks old. There are people who will say that your baby can hear when it is born and others who will say it can't because its ear canals are filled with fluid. All this leaves parents rather perplexed, and they begin to wonder whom to believe. As far as I'm concerned, it is very hazardous to have parents who lack confidence in themselves and knowledge about their growing, developing child.

Most of my colleagues, who have attempted to provide knowledge to parents, have given them recipes, cookbook-style, on what to do and what not to do without ever explaining why. They talk down to parents. Pediatricians may say that babies sometimes cry for no reason, and parents will believe that. How do they know the baby cries for no reason? I think it is much fairer to say that babies are crying for a reason but we don't always know what the reason is, and we should always make an attempt to satisfy that need.

You will find that many babies will cry until they are picked up. People will say to you that, since the baby stopped crying when you picked it up, you should no longer pick it up when it cries. To me it is all the more important to pick up the baby — so that it stops crying. It makes no sense to pick up a baby and hope that it continues to cry.

Some of the myths about babies are unbelievable. There is the idea that a baby can't see when it is born. I don't know how many of you have been parents feeding your baby for the first time and putting either a breast or a bottle nipple into its mouth. You find that the baby opens his eyes wide and looks you straight in the face, and you are rather amazed.

Many experiments have been done, and we know that within 48 hours after a baby is born it will spend more time looking at complicated stimuli, even in preference to bright pictures. For instance, a child would rather look at the front page of a newspaper than look at a bright red wall. Many parents think when they see a child doing this that they have a genius who is going to grow up to be a journalist or a politician, but that is not true. The child simply prefers looking at more complicated things, but eventually he will get bored with that and cry until you modify the environment somehow by turning him around or picking him up and making things move that way. Children want sensory stimulation and they need it;

all the evidence and the scientific literature indicates that this is absolutely true.

What about the infant's hearing? There were studies done a number of years ago by a man named Dr. Norman Smythe at University College Hospital in London. He was a fascinating and delightful man who started out as an engineer, then went into otology, and finally into obstetrics. He combined all his interests by developing devices that mothers could swallow that would transmit the sounds from inside the body that babies were hearing during development. He demonstrated that fetuses at 26 weeks' gestation were capable of responding to an external sound stimulus. The fetus's heart rate would increase when a sound was introduced through the maternal abdominal wall, even when the mother herself was not aware of the sound. There was no change in her heart rate, but there was a change in the fetal heart rate.

There are other incredible ideas such as the theory that crying is good for the lungs. I don't know who has ever studied the lungs of children who have cried in comparison with children who haven't, but I can't see any logic in this piece of information. My only answer is that, if crying is good for the lungs, bleeding must be good for the veins. Crying serves a purpose. It is a form of communication that will hopefully elicit some reaction from some adult in the child's environment. It generally does. Most people have either an instinct or a desire to stop that crying by picking up the baby. But many parents are afraid to because the doctors will say, "No, don't be a neurotic mother; let the kid cry, it is good for the lungs." And the mother feels terribly guilty. She wants to pick up the baby, and she is made to feel even more guilty by letting it cry. This is the kind of information that people have transmitted to parents, and it is wrong.

If the crying child is responded to by an adult, the child learns that it can trust people, that somebody out there cares enough to respond and to pick it up. Remember, a newborn baby is absolutely infantile. You should treat an infantile person in an infantile way. If you begin to treat little infants as if they are little babies or grown adults by trying to teach them independence, or by trying to teach them that you are "boss," they are going to learn distrust. You may be setting out to teach independence, but the baby is going to learn distrust. I think it is important to give the baby a feeling that the world is a place you can rely on. They will get a much better feeling about human beings if, as they begin to go through the period of differentiation, they can begin to recognize people in the environment whom they trust and can turn to.

Letting the baby cry it out, or teaching the baby that you are not going to be there whenever it cries, oftentimes results in a baby who tunes out the world. Children will give up crying; many of my colleagues have said, "We'll teach your baby to stop crying." All too often, I've seen babies who have not only stopped crying, but have stopped looking their parents straight in the face, have stopped playing with objects, and have even given up the few words that they have learned to speak before. You may find that these children immerse themselves in the only mechanism of defense at their disposal at that time, which is also the most primitive mechanism; that is, denial in fantasy, a sort of schizophrenic type of defense. So, if you want to teach your child that kind of mechanism of defense in face of stress, let it cry for long periods of time. Make the child realize that people out there are not going to answer its cries whenever it has a need, and you will leave the child vunerable to this kind of solution to its problems.

It may sound rather harsh for me to point it out in this way, but I think that if parents ask, we should just explain this kind of information and let them decide for themselves. Then they will understand why they should or shouldn't pick up the baby. What I'm trying to point out to you is that parents are intelligent enough to make these decisions, provided they have an understanding of the behavioral process and not just a recipe of what to do or what not to do. With a recipe, it is just a matter of keeping score: ten of my friends say pick the baby up, three say don't. Then I decide on the basis of these ridiculous numbers.

There is another idea that people perpetuate. Many parents notice on day four, just before they go home, that the baby smiled. The mother is all excited, and she says to the pediatrician, "My baby smiled." The pediatrician looks at her and says, "It's gas." Now I think we've all experienced gas, and the experience doesn't make me smile. I don't know if it makes you smile, or where this idea comes from, and yet people accept it as a fact.

I'm inclined to think that the reason the baby smiles is because it has been satiated, it's happy. Many parents have noticed that the baby smiles while it is nursing. This could be an inborn tendency babies have to retract the facial muscles and release the suction on the breast which takes the form of a smile. This may be a rudimentary physiological reaction that later takes on an emotional significance because the baby learns that people smile back at a smiling baby.

Infant Exploration and Socialization

As the baby becomes more socialized, it may smile at you to elicit your smile. You may think that the baby is smiling at you when, actually, in the baby's mind, it is making you smile by doing something itself. Babies are very egocentric. They think they are at the center of the universe. So when the baby smiles and his mother smiles back, the baby may get the idea that he can make her smile by smiling at her. When a baby reaches eight or nine months of age and starts crawling around and getting into mischief, the parents may say, "No, you must not touch that glass ashtray." You may find two or three days later that the child comes to you, smiles first, and then goes over and touches that ashtray. They think they can make everything all right by making you smile and then committing the crime, which is rather fascinating.

This is why I think it is important to teach parents the language of behavior. Behavior is a form of language, it is a form of nonverbal communication, and, unfortunately, parents don't know the grammar of the baby's language. Oftentimes, parents are inclined to interpret what the child is doing in terms of how they feel about it. For example, take a baby sitting in a high chair who is able to grasp things. Even when they are very young, babies can grasp. If you put your hand in theirs, they automatically grasp. But they can't let go. They don't have the release mechanism developed yet. When they eventually develop the capacity to release, they are fascinated because they can release and things fall; when things fall, they make a noise. Not only does the object make a noise, but mother makes a noise, too. And it changes the expression on her face, it changes the color of the rug, and it causes all kinds of marvelous things to happen. The child gets a terribly great sense of mastery. "Look what I can do to the environment, and look what happens," and the child smiles.

The mother thinks that the child is destructive, and that it is smiling, enjoying this kind of destructiveness. So the parent becomes firm, and says, "No, no, no," and gives the child another cup of milk. Obviously, the child will take that cup of milk and drop it again, and smile again, simply because the same configuration of events took place the second time. The parent may express great indignation, and be very angry, and again hand a cup of milk to the child. The child looks at the mother and looks at the milk, and this time drops the milk while looking the mother straight in the face to see what is going to happen. Now, any intelligent parent would begin to feel that what that child is out to do is make life miserable. The child may be a psychopath, it may be a bad seed, it may turn out to be a juvenile delinquent, and so on. That is how the parent interprets this behavior.

The child is fascinated with the fact that not only can he do something that has all these marvelous sequelae, but also they happen every single time he does it. This makes him feel that the world is organized, that it's predictable, and then he may give it up. I have found, in watching little children engage in dropping behavior, that after dropping things and finding that things go down, children will sometimes drop something and look up. Children probably wonder why things go down, why they never go up. Eventually they realize that, when you release something, it goes down, so they eventually grasp the concept of gravity. That's probably what they are interested in.

Children are trying to find out what makes the world the way it is. If they have a sense of trust in you, if you've been a gratifying parent, you will find when you begin to set limits later on, somewhere around six, seven, eight months, the child will feel secure and not threatened. In other words, when you begin to establish rules and regulations that are understandable to the child, and you do it in a consistent way, the child will begin to feel that he can understand the world better, that it is predictable, and that you will help him understand reality.

I would not advise, however, that you let your child spill milk all over the rug just to experiment with gravity. Instead, take the milk away and channel his curiosity by giving him, say, a rubber toy to drop; smile and let him know that he can drop the toy. I try to urge parents not to stifle this response, but to make it a social response, an acceptable response, so that the child's curiosity and interest in the environment is stimulated at the same time he is learning to go out into the world and do socially acceptable things. We can begin to socialize children at a young age without interfering with their curiosity and their exploratory behavior.

We need confident parents. To me, the best parent is a confident parent, and we can undermine parents' confidence very easily. I see this with parents who feel they have to hire a baby nurse to take home with them as soon as they have had a baby. The parents feel they are neglecting their children if they don't have the advice of this great expert. The nurses usually see their role as keeping the baby away from the mother and father, keeping it clean and quiet, and also conveying how much they know about raising babies. They generally undermine a parent's confidence, and stress the wrong things.

Parents have to begin to look upon their role in relation to their children as important. If you need help and can afford it, get someone who will take care of you, so that you can take care of your child. It is far better to get someone to clean your house and do your shopping, cooking, and other tasks.

A Philosophy of Child Rearing

The philosophy of child rearing that I have acquired over years of observation and with the help of scientific knowledge is that we are trying to create people in this world who have the capacity to love. We want to develop people who can form deep-rooted attachments to other human beings in a meaningful way so that they are capable of love, so that they know what it is. It is important to them, and they can respect the desire of other people to have this kind of feeling for each other. At the same time, we want to create people who respect the rights of others. We want to develop human beings who recognize that they have a role in society and that this can be used in a constructive way.

If this is what we want to do, we can see that the feeling of love must come in the first year of life through a very strong dependency need. If we foster a strong dependency need between an infant and its parents during the first three to six months of life, the child develops a feeling of love and trust. After this deep dependency and this deep feeling of love are established, we have to help the child begin to utilize his own resources for coping so that we can help him achieve independence. In other words, we need to help children realize that the world is an organized place, to help them become disciplined, to help them learn to cope with their frustrations, using their own resources and abilities. Eventually, they are able to achieve independence from this dependent relationship so that they are cognizant of the world and of the rules and regulations. To me, this is the only way to do it.

Most of the theories of child rearing in the past have fostered either one extreme or the other. One extreme says, "Let's not frustrate babies at all; don't interfere with them at all. When they do anything and you stifle that activity, you will be interfering with their creative ability." To my way of thinking, this is not constructive. It doesn't help the child understand the world it is going to live in.

The other extreme says, "Let's set these kids straight at the beginning. Don't let them become dependent upon you, because if they become dependent upon you, you are going to have to help them become independent. So, why go through that whole business? Let's keep them from that dependency." I think this is what happens in organized situations, such as day care centers for infants or communal setups. These children don't have the opportunity of relating deeply to one person in their lives and establishing a strong dependency.

We help children get a feeling of love and a feeling of trust in one or two human beings in their lives and then help them extricate themselves from this by using their own resources. This is what we call healthy ego development. As they become more and more independent, we have to begin to recognize that the parents' primary role in life is to render themselves useless. It may sound a little strange, but I think successful parents are those who have rendered themselves useless to their offspring. That means their children are now able to utilize their own resources and go off into the world independently.

There are many parents who, when their children become adolescents and young adults, cling to them. The parents are always finding excuses for not letting their children go: they are going to get into trouble, they don't know enough, they are not mature enough, etc. Parents usually have two roles in life. They are mothers or fathers, and they are also wives or husbands. When one begins to relinquish the role of parent, life is then built around the other role, husband or wife. There are some people who would prefer not to go back to that kind of role, because of problems they may have had that they could push aside by making the parent role the primary occupation in their marital lives. They are not ready to relinquish the child and go back to that.

PARENT EDUCATION

I have begun to focus my activity at the New York Hospital–Cornell Medical Center on parent education simply because I feel this is the way we can do the most to prevent the development of emotional disturbances. Let me outline some of the programs that I've set up in the past few years.

I began to take over the function of talking to all the new mothers right after they had their babies. I now hold one-hour sessions twice a week. We bring the mothers from all the floors together, and I tell them I'm there to answer any questions they may have about taking their babies home or about the problems they may encounter, and to give me an opportunity to describe certain important concepts in the behavior of a newborn infant and in child development.

When a baby is born, it can see, it can hear, it can smell, it can taste, it can feel. It is highly responsive to the environment, and it needs to have you there to satisfy its needs, because it can't get up by itself and go to the refrigerator for a bottle of milk. It can't turn on the television set or the record player when it's bored. I can at least get across the idea that there is such a thing as boredom for a newborn baby. I also discuss with the mothers ways in which to get fathers involved, because I think it is crucially important to involve fathers in child rearing.

Another program we have initiated is what I call a first-year-of-life series. I meet with couples, 15 couples at a time, who have just had their babies. I encourage the parents to bring their babies along. We meet for two-hour sessions when the baby is approximately 4 weeks of age, 4 months of age, 8 months of age, and 12 months of age. I consider those to be the critical periods.

The first four weeks of parenthood, of course, is the shakedown period, when they have begun to realize what they had not realized before: that babies cry in the middle of the night, and you have to wake up and do something about it. It begins to put stress on the marriage, and the parents begin to think, my God, I've got a problem, only to come to class and find out that 14 other couples are having exactly the same problem. Most people don't know that. They think that they are the only ones in the world with a problem. So, part of the purpose of the group is to give them an opportunity to find out what other people are experiencing, while they are learning what to expect of their child's behavior.

I have just completed work with three such groups of 15 couples, so we have 45 babies we have followed through the first year in this way. None of them has any symptoms of disturbed behavior, although obviously it is too early to say. The parents feel very confident; they feel as if they know a lot more than they would have otherwise, and I feel that one of the values of the program was that it gave them confidence throughout.

The third program that I've initiated recently is one in which I teach 13-year-old children about the responsibilities of parenthood. I've found that telling new mothers it is best to plan their children three years or more apart makes for an uncomfortable situation. They say, now you're telling me. They have two-year-olds at home while I'm explaining what a two-year-old is like and what it would be like to take a baby home to a two-year-old who is going through a normal stage of being defiant and miserable. I decided that maybe we ought to get some of these ideas across even before young people consider the role of parenthood.

I'm trying to persuade the 13-year-old children I'm working with to consider not having children. In other words, I'm asking them to consider alternatives to being parents, unless they are able to recognize how important babies' developmental needs are and how much responsibility is involved in caring for them. I urge them not to compromise the early emotional development of children for other things that they as parents may want in life.

There may be many, many people who should have careers rather than take on parenthood as a role. I think that people in our culture have been brainwashed into thinking that parenthood is the ultimate gratification and the ultimate in maturity. I happen to enjoy parenthood; it happens to be one of the great joys in my life, but I don't feel that everybody else should feel the same way. I feel that there are many people who don't like it, who are not geared for it, and whose past experience does not lead them to be the kind of parent that could meet the emotional needs of children. That is one reason that I'm teaching these 13-year-olds about parenthood.

Another reason is that, in the event that they do become parents, I can at least familiarize them with some of the important concepts, and can describe the interactions between little babies and grown children with their parents. A third reason is that possibly, by having these sessions, they will become much more sensitive to their own parents.

To give you an example of what we do, we discuss what a parent should do under certain circumstances. These kids come up with all sorts of marvelous solutions that would benefit children in their position. I say, "Now pretend that you're the parent, and you have just caught your 13-year-old stealing a dollar from your wallet. What are you going to do?" We debate the issue, and they sit there absolutely perplexed and admit that they don't know what to do. When they ask what I would do, and I admit that I don't really know either, they begin to understand that it's rough. Then we can begin to discuss some possible solutions and what they mean.

These young teen-agers are now beginning to look upon their own parents with greater compassion, and they look upon parenthood as a far more important role than they had thought it was before. There are all kinds of questions and concepts that we try to get across in these classes, but the most important thing we do in this program, and in the other programs, is teach people about the importance of parenthood at a high level. That is, we don't talk down to people.

THE HOPE OF THE FUTURE

It is my deepest conviction that we must meet the needs of children in our society as they develop. We cannot hope to make this a better world in the future unless we can fulfill our children now. Parents have the capacity to create loving human beings who are productive in society; they also have the capacity to create destructive human beings who commit destructive acts against society. It is no mystery when we read about an attempted assassination and find that the assassin's mother has said, it must have been something he ate that day. It shows the lack of insight that that mother has about human interaction. We can usually trace an individual's attempt to gain self-esteem through destructive acts to early parent-child relations.

René Dubos, who I'm happy to say is a good friend of mine at Rocke-feller University, made the following comment: "The humanness of life depends above all on the quality of man's relationship to the rest of creation, to the winds and the stars, to the flowers and the beasts, to smiling and weeping humanity." I think that is an important concept.

It has been a pleasure and a privilege to pass on my thoughts and experiences to an audience like this. I hope I've influenced you to go back to where you have come from and to think about some of these programs. They have been very successful in our center, and I hope that you do some-thing about the problem of parenthood where you work. Your influence could bring us much closer to a world that consists of brotherhood, sister-hood, and peace.

Years of Productivity
and Achievement

Chapter 5

The World of Work — Its Promises, Conflicts, and Reality

Emanuel Kay*

Early in the middle years, work becomes a central part of the individual's life. Adults of this age will spend approximately half their waking hours at work, and the type of work they do will play a significant role in defining their income, life style, geographic mobility, and social status. The working careers of most people coincide roughly with the age span of 25 to 65 defined as the middle years by this conference. Work is important, not only because it represents the most time-consuming activity of adults in the middle years, but also because it provides the greatest lifetime opportunity for individuals to continue to grow and to develop, to express and to utilize their individual skills and talents.

The best way to describe the realities and conflicts in the work situation is to describe the careers of two individuals — a young high-school graduate who enters the blue-collar work force and a young college graduate who enters the white-collar work force. At the close of my presentation, I shall talk about the lost opportunities and the promises that the world of work holds during these years.

THE BLUE-COLLAR AND WHITE-COLLAR WORKER

The young blue-collar worker finds himself in a very highly structured environment when he enters the work force. Typically, he is given the lowest rated and simplest tasks to perform. He receives the lowest pay and has the least amount of security — the slightest reduction in the work force will find him out on the street. When he manages to get a foothold, through seniority, in a company, he may have to wait for many years to advance into a position where he can make use of his best abilities.

I know of a number of situations in which he may have to wait as long as 15 to 20 years before he has an opportunity to bid on jobs in the crafts — plumbing, carpentry — that make maximum use of his skills. What he is encountering is a highly structured system of jobs that increase

---

*Emanuel Kay, PhD, a partner in the Gellerman Kay Corporation, is an industrial psychologist with extensive experience in personnel research, manpower development, and operating personnel functions.

in value (pay) as they become more complex and that require seniority to obtain. For the young blue-collar worker, the reality of work is to find a way to hang in there and get enough service time to overcome job insecurity. The conflict is to be underutilized and to know it, and to have to wait out indefinite periods before one can get to the more meaningful and higher-paying jobs.

The young college graduate, on the other hand, faces a completely different and somewhat brighter set of circumstances in his early working years. Except for the 1970–1971 time period, he generally is sought after by company recruiters, offered opportunities to participate in entrance training programs, and partially or completely reimbursed for his moving expenses. He enters the work force with some rather high expectations about his individual worth and the progress he can achieve in the work situation in terms of development, status, and compensation.

Many new college graduates typically experience some disappointment on their first jobs. The graduate may find that the initial entrance assignments do not live up to recruiting-brochure promises; that he has picked the wrong company; or that he has wound up in a job that does not quite suit his talents or interests. When this occurs, he is apt to find another job and work environment that he feels will better suit his needs. In other words, he is quite mobile. His profession is portable — it's located between his ears — and all he has to do is get onto an airplane or into his automobile to find a place where his skills will be utilized. The turnover among young college graduates is legend and well-documented. The mobility — organizational and geographic — that he has at this point in his career is great with very few penalties attached.

The realities for the young college graduate are that he is highly sought after, paid an excellent starting salary, and enters a work environment he can change when it suits his needs, and in which he can and does advance, based on his performance and ability.

In the early years, we see quite a contrast between the two individuals whose careers we are following. The blue-collar worker waits his turn, tends to be grossly underutilized in his early work experiences, and is affected more by the ups and downs in our economy. The young college graduate, on the other hand, can find the early years quite exhilarating. He is sought after and given opportunities to develop and utilize his abilities pretty much in accordance with his own motivation to do so.

Let us jump ahead a number of years and take a look at the realities and conflicts for our two workers in their mid-thirties. The blue-collar worker has achieved some security, is not as strongly affected by the ups and downs in our economy, and has gotten to, or close to, the jobs that offer him more opportunity to grow and develop and that increase his pay. The college graduate quite probably has entered the middle-management ranks and is earning $18,000–20,000 a year and upward. He has been recognized as an individual who has mastered his profession and who can make a significant contribution. He may have been identified as a person who is a "real comer" with potential for top management positions that hold even greater promise of financial and social rewards and opportunities for development.

THE MID-LIFE CRISIS

We might say, at this point, that both have it pretty good. But, it is at this point that the facts of human psychological development come into play to create some unsettling realities, and both of our workers are experiencing the so-called mid-life crisis. The world of work is not very helpful to an individual at this critical stage when he undertakes a rather anxiety-producing evaluation of his life.

First, he is in a good position to see the realities, and, second, he sees this as a point in his life where he must make a change, if one is to be made at all. Typically, he is looking at what he has achieved to date and what he is likely to achieve in his remaining years in his work career, his marriage, his children, his life style, his social roles, and his friendships. The end result of this evaluation can be a significant change in any or all of the above, and we may see new wives, jobs, careers, and life styles as the result. Some individuals elect to live with their past styles and patterns for the remainder of their lives.

Researchers studying this phase of human psychological development tell us that this is a critical phase in these respects:

1. Most people experience it. It is not an isolated phenomenon.

2. The individual who opts for change will go through several very uncomfortable years before his crisis is resolved. However, this individual is more likely to be the one who continues to grow and develop in his later years.

3. The individual who does not opt for change is apt to stagnate.

I do not think we know, as yet, why some individuals opt for change and others do not, but we do know that a significant number of people in all walks of life and in all occupations experience this crisis to varying degrees of intensity. The working through of the crisis requires, first, that we understand it and accept it as a *normal human phase of psychological development* and, second, that our society be flexible enough to allow it to happen.

Now let us get back to our two workers and take a look at the mid-life crisis in the world of work. The blue-collar worker is fairly well boxed-in. Change for him means giving up his seniority and job security which he has put in a lot of years to get. He has few options within his organization to make significant career or job changes. He may have to go outside the organization to make changes in this area, and probably at considerable risk and potential loss — for example, interests in a pension program. He will get little financial support for career changes and/or geographic moves.

Our college graduate, now a middle manager, is better off in this situation, but not much. He, too, finds that the organization cannot accommodate his needs for change. He probably has come up through one specialty in the organization and is now at a level, in the organization and in salary, where it is difficult for him to move around to get a broader range of experience. In addition, he will find that his job boundaries are relatively inflexible — there are few opportunities to add to his job new work or new responsibilities that will represent a significant change or opportunity for him to express new interests. He, too, is boxed-in by the organizational structure, its manpower management rules, and the possible loss of rights in a pension program if he leaves.

Thus, both men are in difficult positions in this stage of their working lives. They both have intense needs for flexible work environments, but the reality of the work situation is that the organization is very inflexible for them. The working through of their mid-life crises can only be hampered by this inflexibility. Their conflict, basically, is to find a more meaningful work role within the confines of organizations that are inflexible.

Now, let us look at the final stages of the work career. The blue-collar worker has about as much seniority as he needs to be protected from the ups and downs in the economy, and he has access to the best jobs in the plant. For him, the final years of work can be the most comfortable and satisfying, and studies of blue-collar workers generally indicate this. Keep in mind that it has taken him many years to get to this point.

For the college graduate who has become a middle manager and has not made it into the top executive ranks, the final years of work can be very uncomfortable and dissatisfying. He may be cornered in a narrow job with no prospects of promotion. He may feel that he lacks authority to do his job and has little involvement in the decision-making process. He may become the unwitting victim of mergers and reorganizations, see the salaries of new college graduates increase faster than his own, get the distinct impression that his role as a middle manager is not valued, and face the prospect of working in an administrative and bureaucratic morass that does not make use of his skills and that is not satisfying. Thus his final years can be a period of marking time with no opportunity to realize the fulfillment of his abilities until he gets the golden handshake — retirement — the earlier the better.

As we look at our two men, we see an interesting contrast. The blue-collar worker may spend the first half of his career waiting until he can get security and jobs that utilize his best abilities. The latter part of his career is apt to be more satisfying. For the college graduate/middle manager, the reverse is true. His greatest growth is in his early years and, from approximately age 45 on, he is apt to be plateaued and dissatisfied. They both share in common the working through of the mid-life crisis in inflexible organizational settings.

PROMISE OF THE WORLD OF WORK

What is the promise of the world of work? The promise is that the world of work will be a meaningful experience for all individuals, regardless of the color of their collars, at every year in which they are in the work force. As a society, we cannot afford to let an activity in which individuals spend half their waking hours be a source of dissatisfaction for up to half their working careers. We cannot afford to waste this amount of human talent; neither can we afford the by-products of dissatisfaction in our work situations.

How can we achieve the promise of a work situation that utilizes human talent over a long period of time and that recognizes and deals constructively with different phases of human development? I think there are a number of pressures already operating that will help us to get there. Let me describe them.

The Workers Themselves

We have become a society in which individuals are destined to work in organizations. Less than 100 years ago, 90% of the population worked on farms and 10% in business. Today, the reverse is true — 90% of us work in business or services and 10% work on farms. There are approximately 82 million people engaged in nonfarm employment, and of these 82 million, approximately 6 to 7 million are self-employed. The rest of us — 74 to 75 million — are on someone else's payroll.

I am suggesting that we listen to the people in our work force — people of all ages, sexes, colors, and occupational levels — and hear what they have to say. Our young blue-collar workers already are telling us how they feel — they are quite negative and less "manageable," both to management and union leaders, than past generations. They are dissatisfied with the monotony of the work that they must do and many are militantly seeking changes that will satisfy their needs.

The middle managers also are expressing their discontent. They are not as militant or as well organized as the young blue-collar workers. They are expressing their discontent in their own way, however. More and more they are refusing promotions that would disrupt their family lives and more and more they are dropping out and seeking new careers that will enable them to continue to develop and to grow.

Blacks and other minority groups are just getting a foothold in the work force, and they are seeking what our fathers and grandfathers sought — a piece of the action and some reasonable security. Women traditionally have been one of the most underutilized resources in our work force, and they now are speaking up.

There are a lot of voices and constituencies in our work force today. I don't envy the top executives and union leaders who have to do a lot of the listening. These men and women workers are telling us that the world of work is not satisfying, and this is a message our organizations, union leaders, and society cannot afford to ignore.

Top Management-Union Leaders

Organization leaders wield a lot of power, particularly the power to bring about change. The worst thing they can do is to become defensive and to dismiss or rationalize what they hear from the workers. I appreciate that they have to respond to many publics, both internal and external to their organizations, but they must not engage in oversimplifications and denials that we have a serious problem in our work force at all levels. Recognition of the problems in our work force is going to make their jobs more complicated, but then no one ever said that organization life was simple.

Government

Government, at all levels, has an important role to play. Legislative, executive, and judicial actions in the past eight to ten years have been instrumental in opening up many problems associated with work — equal employment opportunities, for example. These efforts have dealt with basic security and employment opportunities. Recently, we have seen legislative hearings conducted around the topic of worker satisfaction. Legislation that would compel employers to "comply with levels of worker satisfaction" is being talked about, and if it made sense, could be another important spur to organizations to deal seriously with this problem.

Educational Institutions

Our educational institutions are geared more toward the needs of youth than the needs of adults. More and more, I think we can expect people to pursue at least two careers. Recent studies, for example, have shown that about 45% of blue-collar *and* white-collar workers would change careers if they could. Now, of course, not all would or should, but if only 25% did, then the needs for education at an adult level would increase significantly. I can think of no better way to increase the productivity of a university facility than to operate it more hours of the day and more days of the week and to fill the classrooms with adults who are seeking learning as a way of continuing their development.

Interested Professionals

There are many of us today who are interested in organizations and the problems of work. We do research, we write books, we give talks at meetings such as this, and we do consulting work with organizations. We've made a lot of noises about these subjects and probably will continue to do so. However, as we go back and work in our communities and in organizations, there are several problems we face. The first is that we may alienate our audience. We find ourselves talking about "them" and for "them," and the "them" tend to get somewhat resentful and defensive. What I'm saying is, we can overstudy the problem and deal with it too long at an intellectual level and lose our audience in the process. We're also in competition with vested-interest groups who feel the problem of worker satisfaction legitimately is theirs. Are we going to compete with them, or are we going to work with them to help them understand the problem that exists and to develop solutions?

Another problem of the interested professionals is they do not have all the answers. We do a lot of work to define problems, but not enough to achieve solutions. Organizations are very complex, and there are many conflicting forces within their confines. We must avoid the simplistic and partial solutions to which we are prone at times and also avoid raising expectations we cannot satisfy.

In summary, the quality of life at work leaves a lot to be desired at all occupational levels. We are paying significant hidden costs in terms of human satisfaction and productivity. We just cannot afford to alienate the growing numbers of people in their middle years who will be spending half of the hours they are awake in our organizations. We cannot afford it in terms of what it means to these individuals, and we cannot afford it in terms of what it means to our society.

Chapter 6

The Role Played by Unions

Nat Weinberg*

The middle years are the years when unions play a major part in determining the quality of life for millions of workers. As you know, wage and salary workers, together with their families, make up the great majority of the population of this country. So the quality of their lives pretty much determines the quality of life in the society as a whole.

Unions directly affect the lives of their members, but indirectly they have a very substantial influence on the lives of nonmembers as well. The reason for this is, I think, fairly obvious. Nonunion employers, either to compete in the labor market or to keep the union out, try to keep their workers not too far behind the games run by union workers, though you will find, if you look at the statistics, that union workers over the long term are considerably better off.

There's one thing that no nonunion employer can give to his workers, and what the employer cannot give seems to me to be much more important than what he can give. As you know, we take a great deal of trouble in this country teaching children all about the virtues of democracy. Yet when they graduate from school and go into a plant or office where there is no union, they suddenly find themselves in an environment that for all practical purposes is despotic. It may be a benevolent despotism. The employer may want to be generous, kind, and considerate to his workers. Nevertheless, in a democracy, it is incompatible with the dignity and self-respect of the individual human being to be dependent for his welfare on somebody else's benevolence.

There is no question that in the absence of a union a plant is an autocracy. The boss's will or whim is law; and if it is not carried out, somebody is in trouble. It's only when the worker has an organization through which he can speak that he can assert his dignity as a human being, that he can protect his interests, that he can see to it that managerial decisions take into account not only the objectives of the business but also his welfare and the welfare of his family.

---

*Nat Weinberg is director of the Special Projects and Economic Analysis Department of the United Automobile Workers in Detroit, Michigan. His current activities include consultant to the National Commission on Productivity, board member of the Project on Corporate Responsibility, and member of the Harvard College of Economics Visiting Committee.

We all know that even when an employer wants to be benevolent, there are drives and pressures to yield to so that the objectives of the business can be carried out, to meet competition and maximize profits. The pressures on management often mount to the point where human considerations are brushed aside, and the worker becomes relegated in effect to the status of an attachment to the machine.

The function of a union is to assert the human values in the plant; to assert that the human being at work at a machine is not himself a production tool, that he is not a means to an end, but an end in himself. What the union tries to do in the plant is to substitute the rule of law, as embodied in the provisions of the collective bargaining agreements, for the rule of men who happen to be in top positions in management. Those of you who are familiar with the operations of unions know that most union agreements provide very elaborate machinery for representation of workers with respect to their problems or grievances. Like other human institutions, individual unions vary in their strength, their determination, and their skill in carrying out the functions I have outlined. I am going to tell you something about what the UAW has accomplished and is attempting to do to improve the quality of life for its members, but first I'd like to give you a brief glimpse of what the average American worker, union and nonunion, is up against economically.

THE AMERICAN WORKER

There is a lot of emphasis today on job satisfaction and the status and dignity of the human being, but it's often forgotten that his status in the community is dependent in large part on the level of his income. The bureau of labor statistics has a broad category covering 50 million workers that they designate with the gobbledy-gook phrase, "production and non-supervisory workers in the private and agricultural economy." The 50 million people in that category, at latest report, were averaging $3.73 an hour in wages. Over a year, if they're not laid off, if they work 40 hours a week, 52 weeks a year, they would earn $7,700.58.

The Bureau of Labor Statistics also computes something called a moderate city worker's family budget. This budget allows $11,000 a year for a family of four. To give you some idea of the level of living you can support on $11,000 a year, the BLS budget allows the man of the family one new suit every four years. It allows the family one new toaster every 33 years and one new stove and refrigerator every 17 years. The budget makes no provision for savings.

In the 50 million worker category that I've described, the average worker is more than $3,000 short of what it takes for a family of four to live at that level. The husband can make it if his wife or someone else in the family is working. Obviously, the quality of life for the average American worker is not very good.

What does the typical worker want during his middle years? First, he wants decent pay. He wants pay high enough to provide a reasonable amount of comfort for his family and savings for emergencies and for education of his children. Secondly, he wants security for his family against the hazards and uncertainties connected with his job and his life. Third, he wants what is now popularly known as job satisfaction — work that will provide some measure of psychological reward during the eight hours a day that he spends in the plant. He wants a job that will enable him to function as a human being, making use of his mental capacities, instead of as a mindless automaton doing monotonous, repetitive work that is often controlled and paced by machines.

THE AUTO INDUSTRY AND THE UAW

Those of you who are as old as I may remember that the auto workers were once among the most insecure workers of all industrial employees in this country. During the NRA period, a report was prepared by Leon Henderson on regularization of employment in the auto industry. That report is one horror story after another about the conditions under which auto workers lived at that time. They had no job security whatsoever. Many of them had to bribe their foremen to keep their jobs. The report pointed out that the companies frequently kept long lines of unemployed men in front of the hiring gate so that the foreman was in a position to tell a worker to hop to it or there was a fellow outside ready to take his job.

The UAW was born in rebellion against that sort of thing. It was born primarily in rebellion against the nature of working conditions in the auto industry and in rebellion against the pace of work called "speedup." It was in the auto industry that the phrase, "too old at forty," was coined because the industry worked people at such a furious pace that by age 40 they were frequently burned out. Then the industry would dump them on the industrial scrap heap.

The UAW had to work on three fronts. First, there was the question of improving the workers' living standards, which meant increasing wages. We've tried to do that in a noninflationary way. The second front we had to work on was economic security, and the third front was improving working conditions. Security is particularly important to the worker in his middle years. Those are the years when he is raising a family, when he's concerned about a steady flow of income to meet his bills and to keep the food coming into the house. Those are also the years when he begins to worry about what happens to him and his wife after he stops working, after he retires.

The first step taken by the union was on the question of job security. The principle of seniority was established so that no individual in the company could arbitrarily discharge a worker. At the present time, we have seniority on a time-to-time basis, which means that if a worker has ten years of seniority in the plant and is then laid off, before a new worker is hired in his place, the first worker has a right to be recalled to his job for the next ten years. If it's 15 years, he has the same right for 15 years. The right is there, if that should happen.

There are many other forms of security needed by workers that we have had to provide through collective bargaining in this country but that are provided in other countries under various kinds of social insurance. At this meeting under the sponsorship of the American Medical Association I think it's appropriate to point out that the US is the only industrialized country in the world that doesn't have some form of national health insurance. In many other ways our social insurance legislation falls far short of what other countries provide. For example, we have to supplement public social security pensions because they're so miserably low. In relation to wages, they're about half as high a percentage of wages in this country as they are in Germany or Sweden. Under our pension programs we've provided survivor benefits for the spouses of the workers, whether they be male or female.

In the health insurance field, we cover not only the worker but his family, the retired workers and their spouses, and survivors. A laid-off worker may continue to be covered for up to a year, and we have one of the best and most comprehensive collective bargaining health insurance programs anywhere in the country. It covers hospitalization, surgery, medical care, and prescription drugs. For any prescription, our members don't need to pay any more than $2, and we have arrangements in many places where it costs them only $1.07 for a month's supply. Our program also includes mental health care, which is very important for blue-collar workers. It's been shown that blue-collar workers are subject to more mental health problems proportionately than other segments of the population.

We have to supplement a miserably inadequate public unemployment insurance program through what we call supplemental unemployment benefits. All of these benefits that I am talking about are paid for fully by the employer. We provide life insurance that runs from about $10,000 to $14,500 depending on the worker's wage, and in addition to lump-sum life insurance, the worker's family is entitled to so-called transition benefits of $175 a month for the next 24 months after the worker's death. In addition, if a worker leaves a widow who's let's say, 48 years old or older when he dies and therefore has little opportunity for getting a job, there is a bridge benefit that will carry her over to age 62 when she can qualify for social security pensions. That also amounts to $175 a month. On these insurances, the worker is also covered for as much as a year after he's laid off.

We have weekly sickness and accident benefits, which are common in other countries but which are available in only four or five states in this country. We have extended disability benefits. If a worker is still disabled after receiving 52 weeks of sickness and accident benefits, he can get from $350 to $590 a month, depending upon his wage for a period of time equal to his seniority in the company minus the year for which he has received weekly sickness and accident benefits. We're going to try to improve all these programs in this year's negotiations, and we expect to add a death insurance program as well.

We think collective bargaining is the wrong way to provide insurance for several reasons. First, insurance provided through collective bargaining means that a large part of the population is left without coverage. Second, where there are no unions or where unions are weak, the coverage is mostly inadequate. Third, the security of the worker and his family is tied to the continuance of his employment relationship. If he loses his job, all that security is gone except his pension. The corporations complain bitterly about rising costs of medical care and other insurance that they have to bear, but they refuse to join with us in battling for national health insurance.

JOB SATISFACTION AND WORKING CONDITIONS

The question of job satisfaction and working conditions has always been a major issue for the UAW, even though it has only recently become a fad for the academics, the journalists, and some people in government. It was dramatized, I suppose, by the Lordstown strike. I'd like to put that into perspective. Only two things were unique about the Lordstown strike: first, the average age of the workers — about 24 years old; second, despite low average age and lack of experience with unionism, the workers behaved like seasoned unionists.

Lordstown was not a wildcat strike. We are one of the few unions in this country that preserves the right, during the life of the contract, to strike over certain working conditions, such as work pace and health and safety matters. The Lordstown strike attracted a great deal of attention, but not very many miles away in Ohio there was another strike in an old plant with older workers that lasted for 172 days over identical issues. That was the longest strike in General Motors history, and it received practically no attention whatsoever.

We have these strikes every year, because every time a new model comes in, the corporations try to squeeze more work out of the workers by accelerating the work pace.

On the question of working conditions, I'd like to read to you something that was said in a resolution adopted by our convention back in May 1966, long before the current fad.

> Human labor is not simply another economic resource like machines or materials to be bought as cheaply as possible and used as efficiently as possible. People at work do not check their humanity at the plant door. The cold calculus of efficiency must be mitigated by consideration for workers as human beings. The work pace must leave them enough energy at the end of the day to enjoy their time at home with their families. The environment in which they perform their labors must be as clean, as healthy, and as pleasant as it is possible to make it. The attitudes toward workers of those having managerial

responsibility must conform to the democratic concept of the worth and the dignity of every individual. Jobs must be adapted to the physical and mental needs of people and not vice versa. Ingenuity must be devoted to counteracting and reversing the tendency of advanced technology to deprive work of its creative and rewarding content. Imaginative new ways must be found to enable workers to participate democratically in decisions affecting the nature of their work.

This is an old struggle with us. We keep working at it, but there are difficulties. One difficulty is that each operation presents unique problems, and you cannot have one overall solution that will apply to every job in an industry as complicated as the auto industry. Because of this, a great deal of experimentation is required. General Motors will spend $50 million for the right to experiment with the Wankel engine and will spend a comparable amount in carrying on the actual experimentation, but when it comes to experimenting with and improving work for people in its plants, General Motors spends nickels and dimes in comparison with the hundreds of millions of dollars it spends for technological research.

Another difficulty in improving job satisfaction is that labor and management disagree about the objectives of improvements as well as the nature of work. Management's purpose in improving work is to motivate workers so that productivity and profits will increase. We in the labor movement regard job satisfaction, or at the very least making work a little less intolerable, as an end in itself, even if it costs something in productivity. When we increase relief time for the workers on the assembly lines so that they can get a break from the monotony of a car bearing down on them every minute, we reduce productivity, and we're glad we do. The worker is more important than the number of cars that come off that line. Fortunately, we are not alone in saying that human well-being is an end in itself, even if it costs something in productivity. The automation commission that was created by Congress some years ago took the same position, with only a couple of the employer members dissenting.

I don't expect that with these words I've made rabid unionists out of you, but I do hope you will have a better understanding of what unions try to do to improve the quality of life for their members.

Chapter 7

The Development of
Human Resources

James L. Hayes*

If you will agree with the assumption that the middle years are not all that they could be, I will look at the question from a management point of view. When I do this, I am not saying, management counter to labor. As a matter of fact, most labor activity came into existence because of bad management.

Management has been described in many ways. The definition I like best is that management is not the doing of things, it's the development of people. That's not the most common description, which is that management is getting things done through and with other people. The mature, well-developed manager always hears that fundamental with two emphases. The amateur hears it with one.

The amateur hears that management is getting things done *through other people*. "Today I'm a boss; I've got a kingdom, my group." This is what I call the happy school. These are the people who will say, "Well, it is true we're not reaching our objectives, but have you tested the morale of my people?" It's the happy failure concept. The mature manager hears two things always: it's *getting things done* and *through other people*.

Unions are managed, let's not forget that. Social agencies are managed. Universities are managed. Management is a universal concept. But where do managers come from? In very many cases, you look around in your own organization. It may be a social agency, a hospital, a management association, a union. You find someone who is fairly industrious, working on the technical side. You say, "There's a good man; I think he has leadership. Let's make him head man." If it's in accounting, make him head accountant. Social agencies, make him the group leader. This man goes home and says to his wife, "Honey, hey, I'm a boss." She says, "What do you do?" He says, "They haven't told me that yet."

He begins to think about what good bosses he has known have done, and he tries to emulate them. He thinks about bosses who irritated him

*James L. Hayes is executive vice president in charge of development of new programs, projects, and markets for the American Management Association. He previously served for 11 years as dean of the School of Business Administration at Duquesne University in Pittsburgh.

and what things he might change about their way of doing things. If he perseveres in this job for, let us say, five years, what do we do with him? We train him. This would be akin to going out on the streets of Chicago, picking up a young man, and saying, "Go over to a local hospital, try a few operations, and if you like it, we'll send you to med school." You see we wouldn't dream of it when it involves the physical body, but we are putting people and fortunes into the hands of rank amateurs day after day. Then we wonder why we criticize management.

There's much we can do with good management, but many of the illustrations of management are illustrations of poor management. Any manager who's not concerned with people is a bad manager. He shouldn't be seen as typical. Any manager who says the bottom line is the most important thing or money is the most important thing is a bad manager. The only way to improve management is going to be through development and education.

The important part is that we see in this middle management group the imitation of bad management. It's the largest amateur profession in the world. Anyone can be a manager by appointment, no matter how he acts. You will find that many not-for-profit organizations imitate the very worst for-profit organizations without going back and finding out what it is they've done wrong and trying to do it right.

THE GOALS OF MANAGEMENT

In management you are trying constantly to reconcile two things: the rights of the individual and the goals of the organization. People want to work together to achieve something in common for the satisfaction of the team, while retaining their individuality. Here we find a number of things coming into play that actually kill off the joy of work. For instance, many people who want to be individualists still like the security and income of an organization. These people ought to be professional consultants, like a doctor with a private practice. The minute you join with other people, you have to give up some of your rights, but not much of your personality.

Let's go back to the caveman. There was a man roaming around, probably the only example in history of the rugged individualist with all of his rights. One day he came across a cavewoman. They found that to their mutual satisfaction there was something they could accomplish together that was greater than either could accomplish individually. They moved one step from rugged individualism to a family group. They found that out of a tribe they got a little more satisfaction and security, and from there they moved into towns, and cities, and nations.

Always, when man joined a larger grouping, he got more satisfactions, but he also gave up a little more individualism. You and I cannot drive down the road at any speed we wish because other men have rights, and we want to live in this kind of society. The minute we decide we don't want to live in this kind of society, we find this is a terrible age in which to become a hermit.

What are some of the practicalities that can improve management in any organization and give great satisfaction? I think all people hate work, thoroughly and completely. But they love satisfaction. I see people who protect themselves all day long as far as work is concerned — do everything they can to fight productivity, and give you all the reasons in the world why this is right. I believe them, because the way it has been put together is pretty bad. The same people can go home at five o'clock, put on old clothes, work until one or two o'clock in the morning building a new home, and fall in to bed exhausted, but they won't do that on the job. This violates something. There's a difference then between satisfaction and work. They work all day, but when they're building their own homes, they're getting satisfaction, and that's what we're really trying to find when we do good management.

I used to think everyone believed in planning. I don't think so anymore. I'd be terribly surprised if 10% of the people in this room really believe in planning. I think you believe in plans, that's the mechanistic side, the diagram, but I don't think many people really believe in planning to get some satisfaction out of an organization.

Suppose I am president of an organization, and I get all my people together in a room like this. I say, "All right, let's talk about what we can do in 1974." Someone over there says, "Sir, I think if we get busy on such and such an activity, we could increase our profits, by at least a million." Someone over here says, "If we introduce such and such a system, we could knock 2% off our operating costs." Why is it that no one questions the figures — a million in profits, or 2% in reduced costs? Because nobody really cares. The attitude is, if the organization wants a plan and the president wants a plan, give him a plan and let's get out of here; let's get back to work.

THE DELEGATION OF AUTHORITY

Let's talk about satisfaction on the job. We've forgotten about something, and that is objectives. We put objectives in people; that's wrong! Objectives are in teams, in functions. Objectives are the glue that holds a team together. If I am quarterback on a football team, I get the group together. I'm the leader, and after a little talking and looking over the situation, I must make a decision. I say let's go for a first down. Did you hear me? Let *us* go for a first down. Presidents today get themselves involved in situations in which, although there are people down the line who could form teams and do a job better, say, "When God made me, he threw the mold away. There may be another one heading up this function, but I doubt it." On this basis, they fail to delegate authority. They don't form teams, they just work as individuals.

One of the things that is destroying the quality of much of middle management, particularly upper middle management, today is the fact that there is much pressure put on them by a society seeking answers, and the historic power structure has shown that the power is really at the top. There is no delegation.

Let me give you an illustration. The president of an organization joins the National Alliance of Businessmen, and one day they say, look we have a very difficult situation in our city here. We're not giving the people in our minority groups the opportunities they should have. The president comes back from lunch and calls in his vice president in charge of manufacturing. He says, "We have a very difficult situation in this community, and we should do something about it. I've been convinced that the way to handle this problem is to start with giving people jobs. If they have jobs, they will become competitive. If they become competitive, they'll want better education. Better education will give them slight advantages and, beyond the lifetime of everyone in this company, we hope these advantages will help solve the problem. So, I took on five blacks. See what you can do with them."

The vice-president utters an exclamation, which in another setting could be described as a prayer. He goes to the plant manager, and says, "I don't know where the hell the boss was this afternoon, but guess what he brought back? You've got three." So, the plant manager goes to the foreman and says, "You've been squawking about that job. Take one of these men and teach him that job."

Now, the president of the company is the only man in the organization with no future. All the others — black, white, or otherwise — are seeking upward mobility, and so they're all trying to knock off the other group. Watch what that first-line supervisor does. He calls in this black man, and he says, "All right, let me show you how we do this job. You put this piece on the machine like that. You press down on the foot lever, and you pull the hand lever. Try it." When the man's first product is a reject, the foreman says, "C'mon now. Take your time. We get kids in here during the summer that do this job. Concentrate."

Later, the foreman tells the plant manager, "That black man can't learn. Anyone knows he doesn't have the brains of a white man. He can't undertake jobs like that. No background for skilled jobs." The plant manager says, "I've been watching. We'll get him a job pushing boxes around or running an elevator, but we need someone on that machine. Any suggestions?" The foreman says, "I've got a brother." "Well, bring him in and see if you can teach him that machine."

The foreman brings his brother in, and says, "Brother, let me see if I can teach you that machine. You put this piece on the machine like that, you slap it with the side of your hand so it's flush with the form. Press down on the foot lever, and if you'll bounce it just about one inch off the floor as you yank the handle, it will come out nicely. Try it, brother. Beautiful."

I believe this is part of management conflict today. If I love you, I teach you the art of the job. If I tolerate you, I teach you the science. Where did we ever forget that managers develop people? Good management can solve many problems if it wants people to learn to be effective members of the team so that they can do something together.

TEAM DEVELOPMENT

Have you ever gone through that interesting experience on Christmas Eve, assembling toys following easy-to-follow directions? "You take the red wire in your left hand, the green wire in your right hand, you put them together, and the light will come on." No light. I used to go to my neighbor and say, "Andy, give me a hand." He would come over and say, "Yeah, Jim, you take the red wire in your left hand, the green wire in your right hand, you put them together, and then just a spit and there's the light." I went back and read those instructions, and the word "spit" did not appear once.

Good management is man-to-man instruction based on organizational theories that develop teams. If the leader of the team doesn't have that interest in people, management isn't going to work.

Somehow, in management we've lost the sense of people, but good management directs people. If I, as the president, don't get down through my organization once in a while just to tell people I'm there, then I lose feedback. I don't know what they're thinking. Yet organizations have grown so large that administrators of hospitals don't get around to where the people are, the director of a social agency never goes out in the field, and even the doctor just looks at his own patients and doesn't inquire why his nurses react the way they do.

Good management involves supervision. This means listening to feedback so the decisions made with the team at the top faithfully represent at least the consent of all the other teams. I don't think management looks for unanimity in decision-making, but it does look for participation. I believe the middle years could be vastly enhanced in most organizations, and not just on a security basis. I'm willing to be insecure if my boss will listen to me. When he won't listen to me, I'm going to fight for other security measures because certainly what I think isn't going to do it. No one wants my thinking. The middle years of our lives could be vastly enhanced if only we could put enough resources into teaching people the good management we already know. If it is done correctly, we would stop being amateurs.

Chapter 8

Working Mobility for Women

Naomi O. Seligman*

I have a few comments on my credentials, or lack of credentials, in this field, as a female member of the work force. I am an independent consultant in the automation field. I have never been active in the women's liberation movement, and I have no intention of being so. I have lived primarily in a man's world; there are few women management consultants. There are many women in the automation field, but primarily at the lower levels. My own personal frustrations as a woman in business are incredibly trivial. So I'd like to talk about a much bigger problem, and that is the non-productivity of woman in our society.

THE CHANGING ROLE OF WOMAN

The role of woman has changed a great deal in the past 30 years. Historically, of course, there are Joan of Arc and Queen Elizabeth I, but these are not typical stances of women. Until World War II, ours was a rural or suburban society with a high birthrate. There was a lot a woman could do in the home; she had an economic role in society. The farm, or wherever she lived, really was important as an economic factor. If a woman worked outside the home at all, it was as a hobby until she reached about 25. At that point she usually married and her husband's career determined her role in society.

At 25, she probably began having children, and again her role was defined by that. It was a long, productive life. When the children were grown and had families, if they didn't live in the same household, they lived within driving distance. The woman babysat for her grandchildren. She went to visit them when they were sick, she gave them home remedies, etc. The family galaxy was large and close, and the woman had an economic role to play, probably until she was 60. Her career really was raising children and maintaining the family.

I'm not debating whether this is positive or negative, but it really was the way it was. It was this way in my mother's day, even through my

---

*Naomi Seligman is executive vice president and a founder of McCaffery, Seligman, and von Simson, Inc., a firm that provides unique management counsel to government and private business.

older sister's day. These were long and fulfilling careers for many women. Then came the transitional phase, some of which took place during World War II when women went to work. This occurred primarily among lower middle class women, and was not representative of the whole society. In the early 1950s there was a response — an overreaction — to that. All the girls in my class at college wanted diamond engagement rings when they were juniors, and then they wanted to marry junior partners in law firms when they were seniors. It was also the period of time when the birth rate climbed, and 3.2 children became the norm for my colleagues.

After that, houses and families became smaller, people began moving to apartments, and there was less to do in the home. We're all wired to appliances that reduce the drudgery of housework greatly, but housewifely skills also mean a great deal less; nobody's interested. Suburban life became very much like urban life. The family was no longer embedded in the community. During this era, we began to have women with split careers. From 25 to 45, women raised their children, and then they went to work. Obviously, many of them went into low-level clerical jobs, but many of them entered volunteer work. It was an afterthought — a half-hearted career to pass the time. The next thing that happened was a very sharp decline in the birthrate. Most of the charts I've seen show that the birthrate was going up, up, up, forever, and then all of a sudden we had zero population growth. I think society was totally unprepared for this; women were as unprepared as men, or as management, labor, universities, or big government.

The next phase was another transitional one; younger women — having fewer children — began careers in which they intended to stay. They didn't drop out, and they didn't work just until they got married. They had families and worked simultaneously. Half the married women in the US today with school-age children are working. Some of them have long-term careers. They never got off the escalator for a long period of time. There's also an increase in working women who are the sole support of their families. Divorce has become more acceptable in society, as has remaining in the labor market over the age of 25.

The second thing that women did was enter careers more professionally since many of them thought they were going to stay there. They were less likely to accept their husbands' transfers because they, too, had careers. Today there are many women doing this without families at all. They are younger than I am, but the fact is that many of them are going to stay in their careers, and they have no intention of having families.

We women entering the labor market in that transition period, particularly those of us in management, had some enormous advantages. First of all, we were a novelty, and being a novelty means getting people off guard. It was a great help. Second, we were not as threatening as men to most other men in the group. In some ways, we could get things done because we were not as competitive as men. Third, we were probably not as vulnerable as, say, volunteers. We were all sole supports of our families, so we could speak up. We could change jobs.

VOLUNTEERISM

At the same time, the volunteer role became very unsatisfactory for lots of people for a number of reasons. I know that the good lady with her Christmas basket, which was a tradition in my mother's era, now is no longer acceptable as a type of volunteer worker. Government and social agencies replaced many of the volunteers of earlier times. The lady of the manor who has nothing to do except wander into the social agency for the afternoon is really not as acceptable as she once was. She's considered a parasite, a source of tension, and she's not as welcome as she was. She's not going to be fulfilled by the situation, and she's going to be very frustrated because she's not very useful. In fact, she's competitive.

The 40-year-old woman who does volunteer work is not happening as much today; she's now 60. The 40-year-old women with empty nests are going back to work, although the larger part of the female labor market is still in that 45-and-up age group, working in clerical jobs. Then there is a growing number of women who are not going to have children at all.

WORK SIMPLIFICATION

About 20% of women are still in clerical jobs that have gotten more and more dehumanizing. There are nice ways to describe work simplification programs, but I happen to think they are all dirty work. What they amount to is the endless fragmentation of labor. I've gone through large clerical floors and banks where women do nothing but sign their names all day. Can you imagine signing your name for your entire productive life? This is all a result of work simplification programs to fragment jobs into smaller and smaller tasks. It was very much a fad from the 1930s on, and we haven't recovered from it yet. The purpose was to increase productivity, which I'm sure it did for a while. Now, if you go into a ladies' room in one of these banks, it's jammed full of ladies writing to their daughters who are away at school, or doing needlework, or anything to avoid whatever work it is that's been simplified.

I talked to a consultant today, and he told me that these job simplification programs work very well with women, although they don't work well with men. I asked him why, and he said, "Well, you know if you give them a clean ladies' room and some bright surroundings, they can fill out the forms all day long and talk about their children. We can't get men to do that, but women are totally happy with that."

I think that what you are seeing is an attempt to beat the system, and what you're back to is diminishing returns. Younger women who are entering the work force today are not going to put up with this. I'm not saying that men don't have dull jobs, tedious jobs, but simply that the huge number of women in lower-level jobs will not remain permanently satisfied with younger women entering the labor force.

What we have seen is, first, the decline in the economic value of women's work. All that feeding the chickens is just not useful anymore.

Having 1.2 children and watering the window box in the living room is not of great economic value. Second, there is a decline in volunteers, and third, there is a fragmentation of work. Fourth, there are more women permanently in the labor force than ever before, and there is no sign that it will cease. My generation of women were brought up to be princesses, and all of a sudden that was irrelevant. Society now places very little value on mothering.

SOME CHANGES TO COME

There must be some solutions to the problem, but let me caution you that we don't have any solutions. There are steps to be taken that perhaps are worth talking about. First, I think that employers are going to have to face the fact that a growing number of young women are entering the labor force permanently. It isn't a problem of women's liberation; rather it's a recognition of the economics and realities of our culture. The orthodox pattern is just archaic, absurd. Second, we must realize that there is a base, quite a sizable base, of highly frustrated women in their 40s doing various kinds of very dreary labor. I think this group of women from 40 to 60 in the labor force is going to grow larger in the next few years, partly because of the decline in volunteerism. In this society, automation and mechanization have increasingly solved the problem of production, but they have created other problems, particularly for the old and for the very young. I think they are now also a problem for women.

Some new techniques for low-level jobs that women used to do are going to have to be worked out. Work simplification programs are not going to be acceptable much longer, and this endless tightening of jobs is not going to be a solution.

Finally, we are going to have to listen to the demands of women. I find most of their demands distasteful; I find most demanding women shrill and most of what they say rhetorical and silly. The fact is that, as a cutting edge, any group initially facing problems sounds silly and shrill, but we had better listen, because they do represent a change in reality. It is a time of structural stresses and changes that may not be all for the good, but I think that they are inevitable.

Chapter 9

The Conflicts and Frustrations of Blacks that Result in Latent Anger

Guy H. Dobbs*

I think the condition of black humanity, and the quality of black life, have been documented well enough so that I do not need to review the statistics and data for you. I would like to share with you some very personal anecdotes to give you a feel for some kinds of experience that affect the quality of life for me as a black man in the middle years. In speaking as a black male, I am not speaking for the black movement. Yet as a black male, I am inescapably a part of a black movement. Some of the things that I am going to cover involve values and attitudes that blacks in the middle years share, and the realities and expectations that go along with these values and attitudes.

Black attitudes and values have been shaped by the American dream and by Protestant ethics as have the values and attitudes of many other ethnic groups. There is the notion that, through individual merit and achievement, people will get ahead in life, and if they have the ability to do a good job, all good things will follow. I think the conflict in this for black people is well understood. The second thing that shapes our values and attitudes is the perceived rate of change in meeting the expectations that I just described, at least insofar as black people are concerned. In addition to this perceived rate of change, there is the problem of the early environment and its effects on our attitudes and values in the middle years. So, the values and attitudes I am referring to are not related so much to the material quality of life as to the sociopsychological quality of life.

EDUCATION

One of the most important historical values for black people has been that of a good education. One reason for this is we have long seen education as a way to break out of the economic bondage we found ourselves in. We see education as a tool and not necessarily as a way to fulfill man's intellectual

---

*Guy H. Dobbs is vice-president of technical development for Xerox Computer Services. He was previously president of Isaacs-Dobbs Systems, Inc., Santa Monica, California. From 1950 to 1956, he was a design engineer at Air Research and Development Command, Wright-Patterson Air Force Base, Dayton, Ohio.

thirst for knowledge. Almost three decades ago, when I was an elementary and junior high school youngster in a large midwestern state, my mother bussed me to schools in white neighborhoods. There was something that my mother knew that I didn't know and that she couldn't explain. She knew that bussing was the only way for me to get a quality education, and I find it a comment on the quality of life in my middle years that we still struggle over the issue of bussing to find quality education for black kids.

During those formative years, my black English teacher in a southern all-black school drilled me in front of a mirror so that I could learn public speaking — so that someday I could articulate my thoughts as I am today. She knew something else that I didn't quite understand: whatever I became competent in, I had damn well better be able to do it better than a white boy of equal educational background.

When I graduated from high school and was fortunate enough to have a scholarship to college, I decided to be an engineer. My family resisted this notion strongly, pointing out that for blacks professional careers were really confined to medicine, law, and theology. They knew something else that I didn't know: avoid high-risk professional careers; you'll only waste your education and get hurt. So, even though there are more blacks in colleges than ever, I find it a significant comment on the quality of life during my middle years that a large mass of black people, black children, are getting increasingly inferior education. An unsettling, anger-arousing fact is that, just as our black youths are killing themselves in the street with violence and killing themselves with drugs, their minds are being killed in the classrooms of the inner cities.

IDENTITY AND SELF-IMAGE

A second value and attitude that we're concerned about has to do with identity and self-image. I remember, in my early encounters with racial prejudice, one of the protective devices that I soon learned to exercise was the intellectual game of saying, well, being black is sort of like being crippled. What crippled people do is try to maximize their remaining resources, their remaining skills, to compensate for being crippled. You see, there wasn't a Jesse Jackson around at that time to help me know that I was somebody. So most of my generation has had to struggle with this question of identity and self-image for themselves. Normally, people, groups, and cultures have heroes to help them with their problem of identity and self-image. The heroes of my middle years are dead: Martin Luther King, Malcolm X, and Kennedy. That in itself reflects the quality of my middle years.

From these two areas of values and attitudes that I have outlined, it should become clear that my theme is, most blacks in the middle years are angry. I don't believe that it is necessary for them to have suffered the deprivations of the ghetto to acquire that anger. One of the difficulties of this kind of anger, in terms of the productivity of a whole people and a whole resource, is that it causes that resource to be wasted and used in dysfunctional ways.

I have listened to the comments of a previous speaker on the dehumanizing and alienating effects of technology. Technology does not dehumanize people. Black people were dehumanized long before computers were invented. People dehumanize people. If we are to alter the quality of life during the middle years, we are going to have to find some different techniques for involving and resurrecting genuine concern about people, both black and white. The thing that makes me angry as a black man is that I do not feel that there is any sense of commitment or care on any broad scale in this majority culture in which I find myself. I think that expresses the quality of my middle years.

Discussion

MODERATOR

John O. Alexander, vice president of the Professional Institute of the American Management Association.

PANELISTS

J. Thomas Cathcart, senior vice president of Eastern Gas and Fuel Association in Boston, Massachusetts.

Claude Nowakowski, chief counselor for the Community Services Committee of Local 65, United Steelworkers of America in Chicago.

Robert N. McMurry, president of the McMurry Company with offices in New York, Chicago, and Los Angeles, and affiliates in London and Sydney.

Irwin E. Klass, PhD, communications consultant to the Illinois State AFL–CIO, the Chicago Federation of Labor and Industrial Union Council, the Teamster Joint Council, and the Chicago Building Trades Council.

JOB SATISFACTION

Mr. McMurry: One of the most important factors in the quality of life during the middle years is vocational placement or misplacement. Management does not always recognize the enormous differences among people — not only in their competence, their skills, their schooling, their intelligence, but even more in their goals, in what they want out of life.

In selecting people for jobs, management generally emphasizes skills, technical expertise, and competence, but rarely considers individual values and expectations. Frankly, because of vocational misplacement, many people are not only unhappy, but also physically damaged by their jobs. For example, the prevalence of heart trouble and alcoholism today indicates in part, that more serious consideration should be given to what a person wants to do, to what extent his occupation will satisfy his basic values and his underlying expectations.

Comment: As pastor of a large Catholic parish in northwest Chicago, I find that job dissatisfaction is a serious cause of tension, worries, frustrations, and problems for my parishioners. Besides individual counseling in crisis situations, what can the church do to help people with job dissatisfaction?

Mr. Hayes: Many problems that lead to frustration and even conflict arise out of dissimilarities in our value judgments. It used to be that if a man walked out of a plant with a handful of tools, it was stealing. Everyone knew the word, and they knew that stealing was a sin. Today, a man walks out with a handful of tools and it's adjusted compensation. You've got to prove he was stealing them, and then he says, "I wasn't paid enough," which may be exactly true. Therefore, he takes morality into his own hands when he decides whether he has the right to that or not as a fringe benefit.

The church could update its ideas of morality. We need normative values by which to judge our actions. I do not agree at all that each man determines his own normative values. I think he makes his own conscience, but that's another thing.

The second thing the churches could do would be to prepare people for rapid change. Suppose churches took up the issue of preparing people for upward mobility. Churches actually should be getting deeper into continuing education activities.

Mr. Weinberg: If dissatisfaction is inherent in the job, people outside the plant are treating the symptoms, not the cause. The union proposed some years ago to one of the big three auto manufacturers that they experiment with having workers on the assembly line work down the line in teams and build a whole car, instead of being confined to one station doing a single operation all day. We said we didn't know whether that would improve the situation or not, but that experimentation was necessary. That's where you get resistance from management, because if it doesn't work, it's going to cost something.

Mr. McMurry: I suspect that a certain amount of dissatisfaction with jobs is actually a displacement of the dissatisfaction with life in general. For example, I recently talked with a man who was full of complaints about his job, the equipment, and the working conditions. After he talked these out, he said, "You know, it's a lousy world." I asked, "What do you mean?" "Well, if you had the problems I've had with a no-good brother-in-law who stays at my house, eats my food, drinks my liquor, and I can't get rid of him. . . ." I think this was the real root of his dissatisfaction on the job. The church could provide an outlet for some of these dissatisfactions. You can't correct them but at least you can let him talk them out.

Comment: What are the positive values in working for a living, aside from the need to earn a living? We haven't spoken of this.

Dr. Klass: There are some 3 million people in the so-called skilled construction trades, and many more in the mechanical trades. These people start apprenticeship at the age of 18, and when they're through, in four or five years, they're just reaching the middle years, as we've defined them. If you ask these people about their job satisfaction, they have it. They have a skill. They have a trade. There are others, too, in factories and elsewhere, but these people are rarely asked about their work in these studies, at least not in my reading.

Mr. Nowakowski: Although I am with the steel workers, my main function is not negotiating contracts or even dealing with procedures or conditions in the plant. I serve on a committee that is interested mostly in the out-of-plant problems of members and of people in the community. We are called the soup-to-nuts committee because we serve anybody who has any financial-assistance problems — problems with welfare, food stamps, unemployment compensation, etc. We are not professionals, and we do not know all the answers, but we have a referral department that helps people find the proper public and private agencies offering the services they are seeking.

About the only interplant communication I have with management is serving on a joint management-labor alcoholic committee. Management has finally come to understand that it is absolutely wrong to fire a man because he has a drinking problem and doesn't know it. Management now sends problem drinkers to the community services committee, and we refer them to either a hospital or an Alcoholics Anonymous group so that they can restore themselves to sanity and return to their jobs.

Comment: I'm a psychiatrist, and I was formerly physician in charge of personnel for an organization with 50,000 employees. I feel that management has a tremendous stake in what happens to employees Has management considered maintaining a hot-line service for troubled employees or a medical service not run by the employer where people could go for counseling in a personal and private way?

Mr. Alexander: There are many companies doing this, Xerox, for one. However, setting up a system for problem solving should not be done to the exclusion of training better managers, and thereby preventing problems in the first place.

When I was working in education, I would have a professor say to me, "Dean, I know you're working on this problem. Would you let me help you?" I didn't really think that he could help much, but I gave it a try. I often found he could solve the problem. It was only upon reflection that I understood why he should have been able to solve it — because he created it. What I am saying is that often this counseling process helps a person identify the problem he has created, and when he solves it himself, he gets a glow out of it. I think it's just enlightened management.

LABOR-MANAGEMENT RELATIONS

Comment: Why do representatives of labor and management always put themselves in adversary positions rather than meeting together as equals to solve the problem of making work more creative while maximizing productivity? It sounds as though you can't do the one without endangering the other, and I just don't believe that.

Mr. Hayes: The adversary position, I think, over time has come from several conditions. One reason is a little superficial, but it is very important in the middle years. All organizations of any kind on either side tend to have people whose security depends upon the continuance of the organization. Now, if management and labor got together, one of us might be out of business, and it's a terrible imposition in your middle years to be out of work.

Mr. Weinberg: Increased productivity may, in some cases, and possibly even many cases, be a by-product of humanizing particular kinds of work, but even if it is not, humanizing work is still worth doing.

Mr. Klass spoke of the skilled worker, the man in a trade who has a chance to use his head. He solves problems, he makes decisions when he repairs a machine or makes a diagnosis. A great many workers don't have that kind of opportunity. They're given some narrow, monotonous, repetitive job to do — turn bolt #56 all day long. When workers ask for decision-making powers in their jobs, many managements fear that they'll want decision-making powers on other issues, and ultimately on the way the company invests its capital. Why not? If the company decides to build a plant over there instead of over here where there are existing plants, the workers may be out of jobs.

I believe people have a strong democratic urge to have a say over their fate. They want to make decisions, and part of the reason for the rebellion that we're seeing among workers now is that they're fed up with being treated like mindless animals. They do want to make decisions. In the automobile industry in Sweden right now workers are being given the right to make decisions about how their work is to be conducted. There's going to be more and more of this, management fears notwithstanding.

Dr. Kay: It's interesting listening to these comments. Everybody seems to want to do something about these mindless jobs. Management typically says, we'd love to do it, but the union won't let us. In some respects, I hear Nat saying, we're interested in this, too, but somehow we can't get management moving on it. We have an impasse here. Are you really talking to each other about this? Are you doing anything about it?

Mr. Weinberg: In the first place, management tries to conduct experiments behind the union's back. Here we are, the legal representatives of the workers. When management attempts to go over our heads, the experiments fail. Second, many of management's experiments are not designed to give workers genuine participation in their jobs, but a phony sense of participation. They're trying to con the workers into serving management's purposes, and workers catch on sooner or later. Third, there is a divergence of objectives, as I said before. Management is interested in motivating workers, stimulating them to increase productivity so that profits will increase. We are interested in correcting bad job situations even if correcting them means some loss of productivity.

Back in 1961, we struck General Motors for some weeks in what *Time* magazine contentiously called toilet strikes. Theoretically, we had agreed to 24 minutes a day off the line for the workers who can't leave their places unless they have someone to relieve them. In practice, management didn't provide enough relief men. What they considered enough men, when they did provide them, was just enough during the first half of the shift so that the first guy to go to the toilet in the morning would have to go the minute he walked in. The same thing happened at the beginning of the second half of the shift. So we struck for enough relief men so that the guys on the line could be relieved during the last three hours of each half of the shift, with emergency relief available when needed during the first hour of the shift. We've been fighting these battles all along.

Mr. Nowakowski: There is unity of objectives in the steel industry now, and a joint labor-management committee has produced a film showing some examples of what's being done to increase productivity through suggestions that come from the shop floor. This film is going to be shown in 18 cities. We have an interesting situation in Chicago. There are four television stations, and we are trying to get the film shown on one of them, but because labor and management are together on an issue, they claim they can't show it because it's controversial.

Mr. Hayes: We seem to lose our perspective and forget that there are far more managements and labor groups that get along together than there are those that make journalistic fodder.

Mr. McMurry: Many forward-looking individual managements conduct employee opinion polls that turn up many of the conditions that have been mentioned. Management, not infrequently and on its own initiative, does correct them.

Mr. Alexander: When we talk about productivity and sacrificing productivity to the human resource, we're saying the cost of the ultimate product has to go up and that the guy who's on the other end has to pay more for it. Doesn't this mean that the cost of the human resource for the person himself is ultimately going to cost him money in the products he buys?

Mr. Weinberg: Well, if you look at the profits of some corporations, you would have a hard time making out a case. Be that as it may, why should I the consumer be subsidized when I buy a shirt by an underpaid cotton picker, by an underpaid worker in a textile mill, by an underpaid sales clerk in the store where the shirt is sold? Why should I be subsidized at the expense of the welfare of their families? If some things are going to be more costly because work is humanized, because wages are raised, I think we'll all be better off.

We continue to think of our society as a society of scarcity. We talk about losing a little productivity by giving a guy on the assembly line 48 minutes a day off the line, instead of 24, but we don't talk at all about the loss of productivity that's involved in maintaining what from 1959 to 1971 was one of the highest unemployment rates in the industrialized world. We don't talk about that kind of waste.

We don't talk about the waste that's involved in denying to people jobs that they are capable of doing because of their race or their sex. Many of those people could be far more productive than they are now working in hamburger joints, or in Woolworth's, or places of that sort. We have a lot of leeway, a lot of fat in this society to increase our total output, to raise our living standards, and to humanize at the same time.

A man doesn't cease to be a man or a woman to be a woman, and neither of them to be a human being, when they go into a factory. We talk about an economy to provide for them as consumers, but we forget they're human beings when they're engaged in producing. We have to remember the humanity in that role also.

Comment: *Time* magazine described a strike in Texas by orange pickers as a classic confrontation between the work ethic on the one hand and the welfare ethic on the other. Would the panel discuss those differences of opinion?

Mr. Weinberg: I think I know what's involved. The growers claim that they can't get people to work in their fields because the pickers are able to get welfare money or food stamps. It is a very simple question of what wages are being offered. If a person is offered a wage that doesn't enable him to live decently, and society doesn't create better employment opportunities for him, then the society wants to support him. You don't shoot him. The grower's argument is the classic one against minimum wages and welfare. If we take seriously the lip service we pay to the value of every human being, we don't ask a man to work for wages that don't yield enough for him to live decently.

Comment: I read recently that managers in retail sales organizations have found that even increased salaries do not reduce internal shoplifting. Shoplifting seems to give greater satisfaction than increased salary.

Dr. Kay: I think what happens is that employees develop ways of getting back at management, and it almost becomes a challenge; it's exciting. Scott Meyers talks about the company that tried to put down illegal betting in the plant. Well, which is more exciting, beating the attempt to put down betting or your job? Obviously, finding a new way to get around company regulations is more interesting. For many people, this becomes a way of life within the organization. We shoplift. Management develops new controls and techniques, and we have a new challenge.

Comment: Why does the game become more important than the job? What are the contributing factors in one's private life and in one's work life that would cause that to happen and how can it be changed?

Dr. Kay: Well, sometimes you look at the job, and the job itself may be pretty dumb and uninteresting. It may not require very much of the individual's energy, either physical or intellectual. It's a funny characteristic of people that, when they are in an environment that is not demanding, they will start finding ways to use their energies. Sometimes these ways turn out to be very mischievous. If management gives people an excuse, such as an insulting policy or practice, for turning their energies against management, they are going to do it. When it comes to these activities, we begin to see the best in many of our employees — their ingenuity, their creativity in beating management systems.

Mr. Hayes: We know a way to do something positive about the game of beat-the-system, but we haven't been able to make it really work. That's getting people involved in the organization. They believe they're outside the organization. They feel no hurt to themselves in what they do. This is part of the team-building concept, which we've started on but which really hasn't been adopted. Somehow, I know, when I'm on a team, that if someone steals, we as a team have lost something. Then the problem is corrected within the group.

Mr. Alexander: Filling station attendants were stealing from a large gasoline organization in Europe. The company's technique for cutting down on theft was to have checkers make random visits to the stations. Then the name of the game was how to find out when these random visits were going to take place. So the company cut out the visits and allowed the attendants to participate in goal-setting. One of the goals was cutting down on thefts. When attendants were given management responsibilities for actually operating a small business, the problem almost disappeared.

Mr. Weinberg: Ms. Seligman's comment about job simplification reminds me of a statement made by an automobile corporation executive who said, "We are creating more jobs for imbeciles than there are imbeciles to fill the jobs."

There are two panaceas commonly offered for the problem of the dull job. One is job enlargement or job enrichment. The response of some of our guys to that is, big deal, I've got one monotonous job to do now, and you're going to give me ten monotonous jobs to do. How does that improve things? The same thing goes for job rotation, which is the other panacea. If you rotate a guy among a dozen different, mindless jobs, how far ahead of the game is he? He wants to be a human being. He doesn't want to be just an attachment to the machine. He wants an opportunity to make decisions, to use his head.

WOMEN IN BUSINESS

Comment: There has been a great deal of talk about establishing day care centers to improve the quality of life for the family in which one or more members work. Would members of the panel comment on the desirability of such centers?

Ms. Seligman: I think the real question about day care centers is who's going to pay for them. American industry is not in a mood to pay for new generalized expenditures, and I think that is at the heart of the problem.

Mr. Nowakowski: There are European countries that are way ahead of us in this respect. The children get excellent care in day care centers. Our problem is money. A bill passed by Congress and vetoed by Mr. Nixon would have provided for payment through taxes. And why not? If it liberates a large part of our population so that they're able to pursue careers, if that's what they want to do or what they have to do to live at a decent level, why not? The country gains from their work. Why shouldn't we share the cost as taxpayers? In the event that the costs aren't shared through taxes, there will be increasing pressure on management to bear the cost. One problem we face all the time is that management knows the cost of everything and the value of nothing.

Comment: Ms. Seligman, I have two concerns. The first is the inequality in salaries paid to women in comparison with men in comparable positions with comparable education. My second concern is the silly, loud, shrill voices of women you referred to in your talk. How can we organize ourselves so that we have more power to do something about such issues as unequal pay?

Ms. Seligman: There are substantial inequalities in salary. A study conducted by Louis Harris, called the Virginia Slims questionnaire, documents this. The more interesting aspect of the issue is not the inequalities of salary between women and men in the same job, but rather the inequalities in the level of job that most women hold.

In regard to organizing women, I think one of the issues is learning by example. I'm told that young women today don't identify with women in management. They identify with nurses and with teachers, and that's the limit of their role identifications. I think that the generation of women coming up now will identify with all kinds of roles, so to some extent the process will take care of itself. As for the shrillness and silliness, I think that is the trademark of any group coping with a new reality.

Mr. Weinberg: Under pressure of law and of unions in at least some in-dustries, inequality of pay for the same time spent at work is on its way out. If you look at pay for different kinds of work requiring similar qualifications, those inequalities persist, with possibly one exception. The low-paid professionals — teachers, nurses, librarians, social workers — have been predominantly women. Teachers have been coming up as a result of union activity, and nurses, too, in some places. But when the qualifications of these professionals have been matched against the qualifications in similar occupations that are predominantly male, the pay scales are vastly unequal.

Mr. Kay: I happened to run across some data on pay and women that are interesting. The evidence is pretty clear that there is discrimination against women in the managerial ranks now as far as pay is concerned, but it seems to affect most the women who have been in management the longest. The way I read the data, women who have come into management most recently are suffering less, or not suffering at all. If the discrepancy really reflects the effects of past history more than current practices, then I can read that as positive. For the gals who have been in management for significant periods of time, the discrimination is very blatant.

Ms. Seligman: But you're only talking about women in management, which is a small group.

Comment: I think it's significant to tell you I'm a very shrill woman. What I have to say relates to the role model. I have this insane desire to give some positive reinforcement to Mr. Dobbs, and it's ludicrous that I should be wanting to reassure the vice-president of Xerox. I'm able to relate to you because you spoke of your anger, and I feel that for me you are a role model. For many American women, you are a role model, and I think it's important that you know this. As Ms. Seligman pointed out, we women don't have role models because the women who have made it in the man's world are unique. We saw this phenomenon in the black movement about 15 years ago, and we called those people Uncle Toms. The women who have made it in management seem to treasure their uniqueness in such a way that they don't want us to use them as role models. I'm glad that there is one person up there on stage with whom I can definitely identify.

Comment: I had to reflect a bit on what Ms. Seligman said about women working, and the historical data she presented, because they conflicted with everything I had been brought up to believe. Black women and work have gone hand-in-hand throughout history. I don't think anyone has touched upon that. And my comments have to do with the need for day care centers, too.

In the beginning of her talk, Ms. Seligman mentioned the economic base on the farm and how it changed. Well, black women have had to be a part of this economic base and have had to work all along, whether it was to supplement the husband's income or to support the family alone. We are finding that we need day care centers for our children since we can't stay home with them. We'd like to, but since we can't, we'd like them to be in some protected environment rather than out on the street or alone at home with no place to go.

The important thing is to provide fuller employment opportunities for our black men. In this society, I think black men are a threat to white men, and therefore black women have been put on an equal basis with their men or above them. My educational opportunities were greater than my husband's or my brother's. It was better for me to go to school because I could make it as a teacher or a librarian or a social worker so much easier than my male relatives. Therefore, the black man was relegated to certain other jobs because of his lack of education. I think it's time we changed this situation. As black women, and as women in general, we're going to have to take a supporting role to our men. As long as management and labor provide the employment opportunities for our men — the training, the educational upgrading, and the jobs — we can stay home and rear the type of children that you have been used to rearing all along.

MANAGEMENT TRAINING AND DEVELOPMENT

Comment: I have a question for Mr. Hayes. You said that many corporations are promoting people into managerial positions without adequate training. Management development programs are sometimes a luxury with some of the smaller corporations. My question is: If a man is promoted to the position of supervisor and he proves to be ineffective, what then do you feel is the corporation's responsibility to that man?

Mr. Hayes: Let me make three comments. First, if you think training and development are luxuries, then you have a basic management problem right there. The minute you put management training in the same category as hot lunches and bowling leagues, you're not dealing with a very enlightened management. The trouble is that many small organizations think they can't afford development, and the truth is they can't afford to be without it.

The second point is that many people do not realize we've come up with an assessment-centered approach whereby we can select people who have a very great chance of success in their first promotion. The assessment approach involves peers in the selection of the man they think they could best work with, and the process is carried out in such a way that no one gets hurt. These up-to-date methods are being used in not quite 1% of all industry.

Third, if a man fails as a manager, my feeling is that someone else promoted him, and to penalize him for his lack of success is unjust. I think you should find him some other kind of job, even if it penalizes you, because you made the mistake. There are many jobs people can work on by themselves; sometimes these are called staff jobs. You can also find a change in jobs with a change in location.

Comment: I'm experiencing problems in developing new techniques and instruments for motivating staff. One of the problems that I see is a conflict between delegating responsibility and authority and developing new ways for staff to direct their own activities — the notion of democracy.

Mr. Hayes: You never delegate responsibility. Responsibility accumulates upward while delegated authority goes downward. Authority, as a concept, has changed over the years. When we had a low general level of education, many people accepted authority. Why? Because the fellow above knew what he was doing and the fellow below often didn't have much training or education. He saw that this man was successful, and he said, "I want to know what he knows."

Today, we have education, but our biggest problem is what to do with people who think. So authority today means, you'd better know what you're talking about. That's authority. "You're an authority" is a way to say it. When you delegate authority, you delegate it to a person who knows what he is talking about. Toscanini, for instance, was an absolute tyrant as an orchestral director, but he was an authority, and everyone wanted to play in his orchestra. His musicians took discipline, they took abuse, they took long hours, they took all kinds of things because they came out of the experience richer individuals. When you work for a nincompoop, you're not going to be richer after the experience, and this is part of what's happening in our change of work ethics. People are working for others, and they think they can handle a question as well as those they work for.

How do you solve it? The wise manager uses participation. If I as a manager feel that you've got a good background and know as much as I do, which I think I should most of the time, then I ask your opinion. It isn't that we have a meeting; it's a way of life. I ask you continuously to participate. When you use authority, you use authority with participation. Responsibility belongs to every member of the team. Accountability belongs to only one, and that's the boss.

**Part
Four**

Human Sexuality

Chapter 10

Emotional Poverty: A Marriage Crisis of the Middle Years

William H. Masters* and Virginia E. Johnson†

The dissatisfactions that trouble middle-aged men and women are not new, but today they are coming into sharper focus than ever before. Part of the explanation seems evident: as more people become comparatively affluent and find themselves with free time on their hands, they are faced with a question they often cannot answer — *what do I really want to do?*

It is a question they may never have faced in all their lives. Until they reach the middle years, for the most part, they do what they have to do: necessity orders their priorities — including the necessity of getting ahead in the world. But, with their arrival at the crisis point of the middle years (roughly at the point where the last-born child for all practical purposes becomes independent), men and women face a future in which they have to decide what to do with their freedom.

Unfortunately, for many people such freedom proves distressing. They understand only too well what the cynic meant when he said, "Be careful what you wish for. You may get it." The mother who longed for the day when her children would be old enough not to make constant demands on her time and energies; the father who dreamed of being financially secure enough to allow him the opportunity to pursue the recreation he always longed to enjoy; the couple who believed that the difficult years, the 30s and 40s, would be followed by the harvest years of the 50s — these are the people who suddenly face a crisis they had not expected. How can they find something meaningful to fill the empty days, weeks, months, and years that lie ahead?

These hard-working, intelligent, comparatively young men and women deserve a better answer than the customary one — develop a hobby. Something that simply occupies time does not fulfill the need. And while no neatly packaged answer will ever be possible, it might be wise to examine

---

*William H. Masters, MD, is director of the Reproductive Biology Research Foundation in St. Louis and professor of clinical obstetrics and gynecology at Washington University School of Medicine, St. Louis.
†Virginia Johnson, now Mrs. Masters, is assistant director of the Reproductive Biology Research Foundation and is a member of numerous professional societies.

their predicament more carefully to determine some of the factors leading to the present dilemma. As a contribution to such an examination, a few limited observations may be useful. These observations are exclusively concerned with the nature of the man-woman bond and its role in the middle years.

THE MARITAL RELATIONSHIP

The problem has its roots in the early years of married life. Once a couple decides to have children, certain consequences follow automatically. The responsibility of conceiving, bearing, nurturing, protecting, and educating their offspring defines the parameters of their marriage. Obviously, it is both appropriate and necessary to organize daily living in relation to this accepted responsibility. All too often, however, the successful completion of a full reproductive cycle reveals a fact that had gone unnoticed or had been ignored — that the single, tangible, all-encompassing goal of childbearing is the main foundation of married life. This goal, in fact, often turns out to be the *only* goal shared by both husband and wife.

In such a situation, when the family nest has emptied, what do the husband and wife have left *of* and *for* themselves? Too often, very little. Particularly is this true if the responsibilities of childrearing have been allowed to dominate or to undermine self-expression and free interaction of the couple as man and woman. Instead of enjoying some of the pleasures of being male and female in a committed union, they devote themselves — sometimes obsessively — to being parents. Rarely do they think of balancing the ledger of their marriage, of weighing the assets of successful parenthood against the debits of their chronically undernourished, emotionally impoverished, interpersonal relationship.

The hidden costs of such an impoverished relationship may be greater than is generally suspected. There is the impaired quality of the marriage itself. Both partners become emotionally deprived. This deprivation takes away some, if not all, the pleasure of being husband and wife and inevitably diminishes the quality of life itself.

But, in addition to the penalty the parents pay, there is the penalty the children pay. Growing up in this state of sterile and unimaginative interaction between an unhappy father and mother, children absorb an image of marriage and parenthood that will negatively color and shape their views of their own future as husbands or wives, fathers or mothers. Especially during the formative years of adolescence, young people need from their mothers and fathers some evidence that the responsibilities of parenthood are warm and meaningful experiences, not consuming and threatening exercises of duty. Otherwise, the naturally constructive spirit attending parenthood may be diminished for succeeding generations. Husbands and wives would do well to remember that the quality of life is related to physical and intellectual maturity, to creativity and productivity, to social involvement and contribution, *as well as* their full reproductive cycle, and that these elements are not mutually exclusive. To ignore all else and concentrate almost exclusively on the reproductive cycle means risking a life of emotional poverty during the middle and later years.

Certainly, obsessive parentage is not the only specter threatening the quality of a marital relationship, and thereby the quality of life itself. Previously, the work ethic has been considered a major cultural influence that can prejudice attainment or maintenance of mutually enhancing and enduring communication between men and women.* The pressures of poverty or distractions of privilege, divergent personal goals, educational and economic inequalities, or disruptive domination by relatives, and a host of other factors, may serve to deny, to depress, or to destroy reciprocal communication within a marriage. In so doing, these disruptive factors prejudice the quality of life during the "middle years."

VERBAL COMMUNICATION

Yet there are reliable ways to guide a marital relationship through the hazards of environmental and circumstantial distractions, conflicting interests, or divergent personal backgrounds. Uniquely individual though these "ways" may be in their successful achievement of comfortable marital unity, they all seem to have one factor in common. This factor is the bridge of communication. It can be built upon any valued dimension of life common to both husband and wife: valued as a source of enhancement to them as individuals as well as partners and threatening to neither one.

For example, many marital relationships exist solely on nourishment derived from the common denominator of religious conviction, or from a shared commitment of service to one's fellow man. These marriages continue indefinitely as viable social entities because mutual commitment provides the partners with a stable, nonthreatening platform of common interest — and thereby a basis for communication.

Between committed men and women, the freedom to talk together — to represent self or to listen without prejudice — grows best in an environment of confident, nonverbal, physical communication. Conversely, fulfilling sexual expression develops best in an environment of comfortable verbal communication. Thus, both the verbal and nonverbal aspects of each partner's mature sexuality are ingredients vital to the attainment of improved interchange between two people who choose to share their lives with one another.

It may be recalled that we suggested a specific differential between human sexual function and human sexuality in 1970.† Arbitrarily, sexual function (sex) is limited by definition to physical activity, such as masturbation, partner manipulation, or coitus. Sexuality is considered a dimension of, or a means of expressing, the individual personality. We always express

---

*Johnson VE, Masters WH: Contemporary Influences on Sexual Response, 1. The Work Ethic. SIECUS Award, New York, 1972.

†Masters WH, Johnson VE: *Human Sexual Inadequacy.* Boston, Little, Brown & Co., 1970.

ourselves as men or as women. We assimilate, evaluate, interpret, and project as males or as females. In essence, all material is moved from intake to output through the biased filter of specific sexual identification. Of course, it is possible to express one's sexuality by functioning sexually as man or woman, but the basic component of an individual's sexuality is the identification with and the projection of a specific male or female image through social interchange.

The adult years have been designated at this Congress as the 25- to 55-year-old segment of the life span. The issue then is how best to develop positive values of sexuality and sexual functioning so that their potential may be fully realized during this specific period. If men and women can accept that the most important factor in an effective marriage is freedom of communication, how do the components of sex and sexuality provide opportunity for this full communication between husband and wife?

NONVERBAL SEXUAL COMMUNICATION

If as individuals and as marital partners we are to survive the social pressures of our culture, there must be built into our marriages a constantly available source of mutual comfort and emotional sustenance. In short, when the complexities of this world are too much with us during our adult years, we need respite — a reliable escape mechanism or pressure release. Marriage can provide this vital security for both husband and wife if they will cultivate the most effective and least threatening means of nonverbal communication at their disposal — the sense of touch.

To touch, to hold, to share sensate and sensual pleasure as man and woman is to express one's sexuality nonverbally in a warm, and hopefully, in a sexually nondemanding way. Husbands and wives must learn to touch and to hold for the pleasure and the support that the sensate aspects of touching and holding alone can provide, without automatic commitment of the basic man-woman relationship to overt sexual activity. For only in the warmth, comfort, and security engendered by full freedom to touch and hold can we neutralize the environmental distractions, the conflicting interests, and even the divergent personalities that can be major barriers to communicative interchange in the adult years. This form of nonverbal sexual expression is the one supportive factor immediately available to all marriages, even to those contending with severe forms of sexual dysfunction. How strange that something as natural as the sense of touch should have become so controlled, even repressed, by a society's concepts of propriety; so much so in fact that the inherent value in touching and holding must be introduced as an innovation rather than acknowledged as a basic and familiar form of human reassurance.

The pleasure and security that the sense of touch provides is strongly enhanced if the couple remains constantly aware that sexual communication need not always lead to overt sexual expression. When men and women are mature enough to touch and to hold without arbitrarily interpreting or intending it as a signal for specific sexual activity, such as intercourse, there is available a most important means for warm, rewarding, supportive interchange as marital partners. When a wife can freely ask to be held or to be stroked in a particular way, secure in the belief that her husband will presume that she means exactly what she says, she will as freely signal for intercourse when that is her need. This is a picture of a mutually fulfilling marriage in the adult years. Within such a marriage, there is common ground from which both husband and wife can negotiate their personal differences and face as well the pressures of our society with the sure knowledge that each wants only the best for the partner. From the security of such a platform, the individual thrives and the quality of life is enhanced for both partners.

This emphasis on affirming the values of touching and holding and on the concept of freedom to touch without inevitable commitment to coital activity should not be construed as an attempt to devalue the communication potential of overt sexual experience. Sexual function is a natural appetite, a hunger that is satisfied only to return again and again. As long as specific sexual opportunity is accepted with confidence and experienced with pleasure, this basic form of interaction between husband and wife can only enhance a relationship.

Nor must underscoring the positive factors of sexual interaction be presumed to suggest that a mutually responsive marriage bed is a cure-all for marital discord. What is suggested is that a secure marriage bed does provide both partners with the means and frequently with the motivation to interact from a base of equality in or out of bed. If both marital partners have granted each other full sexual equality, personal interaction outside the bedroom has a significantly better chance to be both individually stable and mutually contributory.

To provide the best possible climate for a mutually enhancing marital relationship that sustains each partner's individual identity, it must constantly be borne in mind that every individual can be responsible *only* for his or her own sexual functioning, *not* for that of the partner. As long as men and women continue to bow to the sexual misconceptions of our cultural posture, men will either assume or be assigned the role of sex expert in marriage. Husbands will continue to believe that theirs is the responsibility, not only to initiate sexual activity, but to provide sexual satisfaction for their wives. In turn, culturally prejudiced wives will insist that, in marriage, sexual functioning remains man's privilege to dominate, prerogative to enjoy, and responsibility to perform.

Men and women cannot share equally in the privileges of a mature sexual relationship until each understands that sexual function is truly the birthright of both — something that a man and woman are privileged to do with each other, not something a man does to or for a woman. Again, it should be remembered that sexual response is solely the function of the individual — it evolves from within. What the partners *do* share is responsibility for their emotional environment, which in turn is an expression of the emotional bond of the marriage itself.

Without mutual cooperation based firmly on each individual's assumption of sole responsibility for his or her sexual function, there rarely is sexual security in a marriage. When male or female fears for sexual performance intrude upon or even dominate a marital relationship, the partners are denied the incredible value of confident sexual expression, which is the very essence of interpersonal communication. Without a secure opportunity for effective sexual expression in marriage, tensions that the partners can accumulate from every complexity of contemporary living rarely have sufficient outlet. Without full sexual accord, couples contending with marked personality differences or handicapped by dissimilar social backgrounds generally can find no common denominator through which to mediate their social tensions, their personal differences, or their natural sexual demands.

THE TRANSITION YEARS

A word about the transition years designated as the decade between 55 and 65 years of age. Transition to what hasn't been spelled out, to date. Obviously some men and women transit from 40 to 50, others from 60 to 70, and some simply refuse to be pigeonholed. What alterations are to be expected in the quality of life when and if we do transit? How does aging affect sexual interaction and, therefore, affect communication between committed men and women?

As we age, there are only two factors necessary for continuation of effective sexual functioning: first, a reasonably good state of general health, and, second, an interested and interesting partner.

It must be remembered that, as every man ages, he may notice some combination of (1) delayed erection time, (2) reduced ejaculatory volume, (3) reduced ejaculatory pressure, and (4) reduced ejaculatory demand.

As woman ages, she may be aware of (1) slowed production of vaginal lubrication, (2) reduction in volume of lubrication, (3) thinning and loss of elasticity of vaginal walls, and (4) shortened orgasmic experience.

Knowledge that these changes in sexual functioning are to be anticipated during the transitional years is only important in that such knowledge is real protection against the fears for performance that develop when uninformed men and women are naturally concerned or even frightened by the onset of any alteration in established sexual response patterns.

Of much more import than public comfort with physiological symptoms of the aging process is public security in the fact that such evidence of aging per se carries no implications that pleasure and satisfaction with sexual functioning inevitably is prejudiced. Subjectively, sexual interest continues at fully appreciable levels, and objectively, sexual capacity continues as an action potential available to the level of need, regardless of the age of the involved man and woman.

TREATMENT OF SEXUAL DYSFUNCTION

Whenever such information is relayed to the general public, the consequences are predictable. With each new statement affirming both verbal and nonverbal communication as the basis of adequate sexual functioning (therefore of critical importance in every marriage), there inevitably follows an immediate increase in demand for clinical treatment of sexual dysfunction. Until recently, however, the public's needs have been ignored. The neglect of those professions which should be concerned with, but have remained aloof from, the problems of sexual dysfunction has been repeatedly emphasized by accredited representatives of the Reproductive Biology Research Foundation. Only last June, for example, at the annual meeting of the American Medical Association in San Francisco, the presumably concerned professions were again warned of an impending crisis. They were told that the general public was finally rejecting the old cultural taboo that insisted that sexual distress be concealed under a mask of indifference, and that now the issue was bursting into the open. They were told that men and women from all walks of life were insisting that professional help be made available to treat the widespread sexual dysfunction that permeated society.

Today, the challenge to the professions seems to have boomeranged. Hundreds upon hundreds of so-called sex clinics have opened their doors in almost every state of the Union. They have mushroomed practically over night, more business ventures than therapy centers, ready to capitalize, literally and figuratively, on the prevailing public needs, and all too often operating at low professional standards or with no standards at all. This rapid turnabout from the previously embarrassing levels of professional neglect of the clinical problems of sexual inadequacy to the equally embarrassing epidemic of corner treatment centers can be viewed only with dismay.

Dismay, yes. Discouragement no. Historically, this type of presumed, professional response to public demand has always been with us. The same problem confronted the entire medical fraternity at the turn of the century. "Diploma mills" flourished, standards of clinical practice sank lower and lower, until finally medicine was forced to police its own, if it was to survive as a publicly honored discipline. Over the ensuing years, each specialty, such as surgery, pediatrics, obstetrics and gynecology, internal medicine, etc., has been forced by public opprobrium to create and support methods of professional self-evaluation and of critical review of clinical treatment programs. Standards of practice have been instigated, first, to protect the patient, and second, to insure adequate training for younger men and women entering each new field of expanding medical interest.

Currently, all of the involved professions face exactly the same problem of how to contend with the combination of monetary greed and essentially standardless therapy created by overwhelming public demand for relief of the symptoms of sexual dysfunction. Treatment standards will have to be created, professional credentials established, and adequate professional training insured, if for no other reason than that an enlightened public will soon insist upon adequate clinical treatment of sexual dysfunction.

The problem is not at its peak at present, but the crisis is on its way. Wouldn't it be better to have a voluntary housecleaning, professionally controlled at the national level, than to have such a housecleaning imposed upon the involved disciplines by understandably vengeful public opinion? Any attempt to secure full cooperation of the theological, behavioral, and medical disciplines in such a venture would be an enormous challenge, but it can and should be attempted.

For the immediate present, all that can be done is to issue a warning and a challenge, not to the concerned professionals, but to the general public. The warning to the public is to check carefully the credentials of any members of the helping professions who are now volunteering to treat sexual dysfunction. The challenge to the public is to demand that these professions make readily available effective treatment of sexual dysfunction.

The social need is clear. In countless marriages, husbands and wives are deeply troubled by the inadequacy of their sexual lives. They are more troubled now than perhaps they were in the past because today they realize their suffering is remediable. But to whom can they turn? Whose therapy can they trust? The general public has a right to insist on having treatment programs that are not only effective but subject to professional discipline and responsive to professional insistence on the highest possible standards.

To sum up briefly, the most effective means of verbal and nonverbal communication between marital partners include the ability to touch, to hold without overt sexual demand, and to give and take with full equality in sexual interchange. Regardless of the age of the partners, without secure communication, there is no true cornerstone in marriage. Without the warmth of a functional marriage, the quality of life during the middle years is indeed prejudiced for most men and women in our society. For these reasons, the public has every right to insist upon the availability of adequate treatment centers for sexual dysfunction. It is the responsibility of the involved professions not only to develop these clinical treatment facilities, but also to insist that high standards of treatment and responsible training programs are maintained by the professionals committed to these programs.

Discussion

MODERATOR

Irv Kupcinet, journalist, columnist, radio broadcaster, and television personality.

PANELISTS

Leila M. Foster, PhD, assistant professor of psychology at the Abraham Lincoln School of Medicine, The University of Illinois at the Medical Center, Chicago.

Donald R. Young, EdD, is currently engaged in group practice in marriage counseling and family therapy at the Marriage and Family Consultation Center in Houston, Texas. He is assistant professor of psychology at Baylor College of Medicine, clinical associate in marriage and family study at the Institute of Religion and Human Development, and special lecturer in the Nursing School at the Texas Woman's University.

George H. Nolan, MD, a Josiah Macy faculty fellow and assistant professor of obstetrics and gynecology at the University of Michigan.

Robert C. Long, MD, president of the National Health Council and practicing obstetrician and gynecologist.

Mr. Kupcinet: I think the public would like to hear as broad a discussion as possible on the problems of human sexuality. Does any member of the panel want to start with a question?

Dr. Long: Bill and Virginia, would you say that almost regardless of age, but especially in the middle years, after one has been married for 10 to 25 years, the critical factor is the interpersonal relationship itself between those two people? There are hundreds of ways that people who care for each other relate to each other. To relate sexually is absolutely essential, but there are many, many other basic relationships between a husband and wife that are terribly important, especially as they go through life in the middle years.

Ms. Johnson: I tend to feel that if there is a satisfying sexual relationship between two people who are committed to one another, then it simply takes its place among all the other elements of their relationship to make it fulfilling. I've seen too many relationships where a satisfying sexual relationship was a missing link, and thereby so colored, or discolored if you will, all the other ways of relating that the discrepancies and the distresses of the sexual relationship had to be coped with.

Dr. Masters: Ginny and I don't feel that sex is the be-all and end-all of marriage. There's no such concept. It's just a hell-of-a-lot-better marriage with it than without it. It's also terribly important to realize that if you have sexual dysfunction, you inevitably have poor communication in a marriage. Time and time again, people come to us in St. Louis and say, "The only thing wrong is our sexual functioning; otherwise, we communicate just splendidly." Time and time again you find that they really have no concept of how poor their communication is. If there isn't the opportunity of a sanctuary, a comfort factor, the place of give and take on an equal basis, namely, the marriage bed, it's desperately hard to have real equality of give and take outside the bedroom. Do we think it doesn't exist? Well, of course, we know it does; it's just darn hard to achieve and maintain without sexual interchange.

Ms. Johnson: Very often, the sexual relationship is a mirror of the whole relationship. This isn't always so, but it frequently is.

Dr. Foster: With regard to your emphasis on the women taking responsibility for sexual functioning, don't you find that many women have difficulty accepting this responsibility, largely because they've had so much negative reinforcement on taking responsibility in that aspect and in other areas of their lives? I'm wondering, too, if you find any difference between women now in their middle years and women of a younger generation assuming this responsibility. Is it harder for the older woman, who perhaps has had more of this negative reinforcement, than it is for the younger woman?

Ms. Johnson: We would think so, and if we were doing cross-sections of the population, we might find it to be so. Interestingly enough, it's not necessarily the age factor, but the personality of individuals that determines whether they can redirect or modify these old patterns of their teaching. A lot of women have grown up not really believing that it's inappropriate for a woman to let it be known that she is sexually interested, but they have had to live by it for so long that there is an awkwardness factor. Age isn't really the barrier to overcoming that. If she gets encouragement and reassurance by and with her husband — if both of them want this change — then it is much more likely to be changeable or modifiable.

Dr. Masters: The greatest thing that can happen to the American male is to have this concept accepted. You know, we always forget the pressures that our culture places on male sexual performance. We have a unit in treatment at the moment and both of them are tremendously attractive and most intelligent people. Both were virgins at marriage. On the wedding night, there was pure catastrophe, because she turned to him and said, all right, do something. When things didn't go well, it was his fault. She was well aware that he was a virgin, but that didn't make any difference. He was male, and therefore he knew. This is our culture. There is no way for the male to know alone. He must inevitably learn from the female, and he must inevitably learn with the female's cooperation. The tragedy of the situation is that not only does the male believe that he is or should be the expert but also the female reinforces this concept as the result of our cultural influence.

The greatest cause for male sexual dysfunction is his thinking that he must do something to or for his partner.

I'd like to reemphasize: we, individually, male and female alike, are completely and totally responsible for our sexual functioning as individuals. The male is not responsible for the female's sexual functioning, nor the female for the male's. This doesn't mean that we aren't responsible for a certain amount of mutual cooperation. It's just that we have no responsibility whatsoever for doing to or for any partner. If you do to or for a partner, you don't have a partner.

Ms. Johnson: We're not talking about moral responsibility, we're talking about the nature of sexuality itself. There are no buttons to push. You can alter your environment; you can alter your way of communication, your expression of feelings, your representation of yourself; you can change your attire; you can change the time of day, week, month, and year; but you cannot go in and deliberately push buttons, either for yourself or your partner.

Dr. Masters: We are not suggesting that if an attractive female moves toward a male that there aren't things she can do that will stimulate him. We are responsible for a certain amount of mutual cooperation, but the male is not responsible for seeing to it that the female is orgasmic; he can't do this. This is her natural function. You see, the minute we culturally insist on this, it means that culturally we are negating any concept of sex as a natural function. If you accept the concept that the male must do to or for the female, then you say, in essence, sex is not a natural function because the male has control.

When we say a natural function, we mean a congenitally determined phenomenon. For example, there are four obstetricians on this panel. All of them will admit, I'm sure, that there is an awful lot that is boring about obstetrics, and we all play our little games to relieve the monotony. I had the most fun, when I was delivering babies, playing a little game with myself. Every time I delivered a baby boy, I would immediately look at the clock and go into a contest. I wanted to get that cord cut before he had an erection. Half the time I won, and half the time I lost. There isn't an obstetrician in this panel who hasn't seen a baby boy with an erection before he took his first gasp. Well, that's sort of a natural function, isn't it? He didn't have time to be taught this. Every baby girl lubricates in the first 24 hours of life. Sexual functioning then is a natural function, and the minute we pull it out of context, we destroy this concept of natural appetite.

Ms. Johnson: If you don't mind the analogy of food at this time, you might think in terms of one person preparing a meal for someone else. Someone can order a meal for someone else. A person can plan a meal, serve it, share it, or anything else, but one cannot ingest a meal for another.

Mr. Kupcinet: Let's use the food analogy for just a moment. What if one partner is hungry and the other isn't?

Dr. Masters: That's a fine analogy, and the answer is, that you can treat sex as a natural function. Let's suppose you came here tonight, and you didn't have a chance to eat. You go home, and your wife has saved something for you. She puts it on the table, and she's waited to eat with you, too. Theoretically, you're both hungry, but you sit down and you've lost your appetite. You may take a taste or so, and you think, gee, I'm just not hungry. Now does this have her nose completely out of joint? No, she may be a little disappointed that you didn't eat her meal, but it never occurs to her that you won't be hungry tomorrow. But if you go home and climb into bed, and you've had a tough time here with the panel, and your wife is a little interested in having sex, you try a little bit, and you find you're just not involved. In the first place, she begins to wonder what's wrong. You begin to wonder what's wrong. You both wonder what will happen tomorrow. You don't treat it as a natural function. It never occurs to you that tomorrow is another day.

Why shouldn't you sit down to the marriage bed the way you do to the dinner table? If you're hungry, you'll eat a little bit, and you'll see how it goes. If your partner is hungry, there's no reason in the world why she shouldn't eat, and you'll be glad to sit there with her and be good company. The same thing applies in bed. If you're not really interested in intercourse, there are many ways that you can resolve your partner's demand without having intercourse. It's terribly important to treat sex as a natural function. When you're hungry you eat, and when you're not, you don't apologize for it.

Ms. Johnson: Nor do you feel that that's a sign of the total demise of your capability of eating.

Dr. Young: One of the common criticisms of your work that I've heard from colleagues and other people is that you apparently put too much emphasis on sex and sexuality. But I think that it provides a really important opportunity for a married couple to think about themselves, and I would guess that this careful attention to the physical, sexual relationship with each other also engenders careful attention to other personal needs that the couple has. I just want to point out the necessity for a couple to renegotiate their personal relationship as they move through different stages in life. Certainly, one of the very critical issues is sexual adjustment because it does provide an opportunity for couples to say more and be more open about issues that are nonsexual when they are comfortable in sex, and vice versa.

Dr. Masters: Dr. Young, I couldn't agree more with what you said. Let me support it by stating that when people come to St. Louis for treatment of sexual dysfunction, we will never take the impotent male alone or the inorgasmic woman alone. We insist we must treat the marital unit. Now, when the marital unit comes for sexual dysfunction, do we treat the sexual dysfunction? Yes, but it is a minor moment, because fundamentally our total concentration is not on the impotent male or the nonorgasmic female, but on the marital relationship. It is the marital relationship that is the patient always, not the individual.

Dr. Long: Would you comment on the differences that you see among patients in the intensity of sexual drive and sexual needs, and the ease of response? Isn't there wide variation in individuals regarding needs and arousal, even differences between the members of the couple? The reason I ask this is that so many people feel that they have to be identical.

Dr. Masters: Well, there's no way that people can be identical because every individual varies within himself or herself from day to day and from hour to hour in terms of sexual facility, sexual interests, sexual responsivity. What is possibly even more important is the fact that sex drives and sex interests affect the sexual response in a very nebulous way.

If we use the food analogy again, the only thing that we think is important, of course, is the differences in appetite, and these differences in appetite vary from day to day. You'll also have different appetites for the different men and women sitting at the table. The only thing that's necessary in meeting this difference in demand within a marital unit is for both to sit down to the table. Taste the meal. You may not be hungry at all, or having watched somebody else eat, there may be an increase in your appetite.

There are many sources of sexual stimulation. Two great ones, from a male point of view, are whatever the female does to him when she approaches him, and, above all, her response to him. Obviously, the same is true for the female. What the male does to the female is important, but what the female does to the male is important for her. When she turns him on, she's got another dimension going for her, and the only way they can find this out is to sit down at the table.

Ms. Johnson: Everyone is the sum total of his own personality, his own attitudes, his experience and state of health, and just how he feels at a given time of day. Each of us winds up with a set of negotiable and nonnegotiable needs. The nonnegotiable ones would be those that, if they are not fulfilled, would bring about some impairment of that individual's ability to function. The negotiable ones would be simply habits.

This example may sound simplistic, but it can be applied to the sexual realm. Take two young people who are dating for the first time. They go to a movie (let's put it on the double standard for the moment) and, with the best of intentions, the male sits very close to the screen as is his habit. The young woman has always sat farther back. The young man has nothing wrong with his eyes whatsoever; the young woman has an eye affliction that means if she sits down close, she can't see. Her failure to communicate this to him puts them in a double bind. First of all, she can't enjoy the experience per se because she can't see. She also can grow to resent the young man. Her resentment is born in part out of her own contribution, because this poor, innocent young man doesn't know about her need and has sat down front out of habit.

This discrepancy can be negotiated because for one it's a nonnegotiable requirement, and for the other it's negotiable. Things don't always even out quite that well sexually, because it's a little more abstract and none of us has had a chance to understand the nature of our sexuality quite as well as we understand eyesight. By the same token, discrepancies can be negotiated on an open basis. Is your need at a particular time vital to your ability to function? Vital to your peace of mind? Vital to your sense of fulfillment? Usually it's negotiable.

Dr. Nolan: What is your opinion of the amount of emphasis that is being placed on sexual problems today? Every day, when I pick up a journal, there is someone commenting on various techniques to solve sexual problems. To me, this seems self-defeating at the onset because, as you said at the end of your paper, people deserve competent individuals to help them in this area. My concern is that there can never be enough competent individuals to help all of the people who are likely to have some of these problems.

Dr. Masters: Of course, I would agree with you. I have no concept of what it's going to take in terms of professional education and orientation to treat what will ultimately be a great demand. Ginny and I have estimated, and I want to underscore the word estimated because we have no real knowledge, that the level of sexual dysfunction in our society is about 50% of all marriages. We tried to be as conservative as possible. Most people that we've talked to say 75% or 85%, and at least two thirds. Let's suppose 50% of all marriages are contending with varying significant degrees of sexual dysfunction and that each of these marriages could obviously be significantly improved if this dysfunction were treated effectively. Even if they decided to come in relays there's no professional facility whatsoever that wouldn't be swamped. The point is we've got a decade of training ahead of us to even begin to have competent authority anywhere.

When you stop and think about it though, things have moved incredibly fast. The first course in natural sexual functioning ever taught in American medicine was taught in 1960. Think about it. The first course ever allowed to be taught was in 1960. Practically all medical schools today — I think there are three or four exceptions in this academic year — are beginning to teach some of this material. Well, that's thirteen years or so, and you think, that's a long time, but the members of the medical fraternity have been able to say, I've never seen anything move much faster — 13 years to change the curricula of the medical schools is pretty fast. You see, it isn't just medicine that's involved. How many of the theological schools have changed? How about the curricula of the behavioral sciences? Doctors will never be able to handle the problem alone, nor should they even attempt it.

Dr. Nolan: Are you saying that what we have basically concentrated on is therapy for the problem rather than prevention of the problem?

Dr. Masters: Sure, but we have to know what the problem is. You know, in the normal course of events, the first thing you do with anything that's new is run to the laboratory. To a degree, that has been done with sexual dysfunction. Then you try to apply what you've learned in the laboratory in clinical treatment, and, to a degree, that has been done. The next step is prevention. We haven't even really started this yet; we're still trying to learn something about treatment, and obviously, more about the disease itself.

Ms. Johnson: We share your distress, I think. Obviously, there are going to be many people practicing on the basis of their own experience, but this is an area in which almost everyone considers himself an expert, especially those who can combine the expertise of experience with the professional background. Isn't this probably better, even if we have to go through this phase, than the way it has been for years when a person couldn't even send up a signal flag of distress, couldn't even seek help?

Dr. Young: You speak of the naturalness of sexual function and sexual response and the differences in appetite that can lead to conflict. Even if most people accept the naturalness of sex, are they able to make that kind of distinction between the psychological demand and the conflict that's raised around it? You certainly are as aware as anyone of how complex and difficult it is to change those attitudes that inhibit sexual function. The question is, how do people change? What kind of educational effort is going to make a difference to people as they attempt to alter their attitudes as well as their function in sexual behavior?

Ms. Johnson: In treatment, you don't presume to impose a basic formulation on people. It has to do with the ability to go in and have people describe their own distress, describe what it means to them, the place it has in their lives, and their degree of motivation for change. In our case, we insist that both people want some change to take place. These so-called complexities are revealed by the people themselves. The so-called secret of what we do is encourage them to depict their own distress, to categorize it themselves, and to seek new patterns of behavior. It's a do-it-yourself kind of thing. They must accept responsibility for their own change. We help them try on new patterns, but these patterns are drawn from their histories — from their daily interactions and from the things that are happening between them on a 24-hour basis. From that is drawn the pattern of redirection. It is their own pattern; it is evolved by them. They're protected by a state of neutrality, which we insist they maintain, and they learn by their mistakes. They do not learn, when they are with us, by their successes. The whole pattern of direction is theirs. Sometimes, our people, out of the nicest kind of countertransference, care so much they want to give their patients something that they, the therapists, would want. This, of course, we do not allow; we want what the people want. Redirection must come out of their life style, out of their value system, out of their own motivation, and that's why it works, incidentally.

Dr. Long: Most of us who work in this field know that the most common sexual dysfunction women have is their inability to climax during vaginal intercourse, and that the most common dysfunction for males is premature ejaculation. I have found in my own practice that a great deal of anxiety is created for both partners if the woman is unable to climax during vaginal intercourse. Is the primary goal of coitus to climax?

Ms. Johnson: The minute it's a goal, it doesn't happen.

Dr. Masters: I haven't anything to say; she said it.

Dr. Long: I just wanted you to reaffirm that the primary goal of sexual relationships is a giving, tender, sharing relationship between two people. Hopefully, climax will occur, but it doesn't have to.

Ms. Johnson: I would take you to task for your word tender, because it may be tender on Tuesday and quite something else on Thursday, and next year it might be tender again. This is the secret, the imposition. To you, sex may always be a tender thing, but we don't try to make it something for others that we ourselves want it to be.

Dr. Foster: We've been talking about the married population in the middle years, and yet as you have defined human sexuality, it takes in the whole of the life style — whether a woman is able to enjoy being a woman as she defines femininity, and whether a man can enjoy being a man as he chooses to define masculinity. I think you started to talk about the whole life pattern, and how sexuality affects the whole life style.

Dr. Masters: I don't think we have too much to add to what was said. We can amplify it a bit. What we're really saying is that one's sexuality, as opposed to sex as a natural function, is a dimension or expression of one's personality. Everything that every individual takes in goes through the filter of his or her masculinity or femininity. Everything anyone expresses is expressed again through this filter. This is why it's so terribly important to have both male and female present when you're treating dysfunction.

No man will ever really know female sexual functioning. No woman will ever really know male sexual functioning. Therefore we don't understand male and female sexuality per se, unless we're a member of that particular breed. What we have to do is develop the tool of communication so that we can interpret ourselves for each other. It's not just in the middle years or between husband and wife; it's just part of living together as a community of men and women.

As soon as any of us, male or female, assumes we're experts on the opposite sex in any way, we've got troubles. The minute we assume we're experts, we cut down communication, and only through communication can any two individuals interpret to each other what the story is. In communication, we always talk about sending, but it is equally important to have a receiver. No matter how good the message, or how well it is stated, if the receiver isn't working, the message doesn't get through. The receiver set is just as prejudiced with masculinity or femininity as is the sender, and we always forget that the receiver is prejudiced, too. If two men are talking together, the chances are you don't have anywhere near as prejudiced a receiver as you do if a man and a woman are talking.

Ms. Johnson: I don't know whether we've answered your question. We are never unmindful of the fact that people who are not in a twosome, or in a committed relationship, or even devoted or committed to celibacy are also sexual beings and are also coping with sexual feelings to a greater or lesser degree.

Mr. Kupcinet: Let me ask the entire panel, what effect do explicit sex pictures have — pictures like "Deep Throat" and "Last Tango in Paris" in which explicit scenes of sex, sodomy, and other so-called sexual aberrations are shown on the screen? I wonder if the panel has any feelings about what this does to our society. Are these pictures what you would recommend to encourage people to find new ways to engage in sex, which for some people can become humdrum?

Dr. Nolan: I can't envision those movies having a greater detrimental effect on human beings than society has already had on the human race in this particular area. Whether or not these movies themselves allow an individual to expand his or her sexuality becomes an individual thing. Insofar as an interpersonal relationship is able to accommodate this type of input, I think it can be truly beneficial. If the relationship is not able to incorporate this input in a meaningful way, then I think it may be harmful. Selecting those individuals for whom the films might be beneficial is far beyond my capability.

Dr. Young: It seems to me the primary issue in the movies is not so much sexual explicitness as it is the quality of the relationship that is demonstrated on the screen. If the movie degrades or demeans one sex or the other, or both sexes, it seems to me the experience is without any educational benefit. On the other hand, if there are couples who can see the movie and get new ideas or feel a greater sense of freedom in seeing the freedom of someone else, it could be of value. I don't know that there are any studies on it.

Comment: I am a doctor and I teach behavioral science to medical students at the University of Illinois. One thing that a medical student showed me the first time I appeared at their sessions on sex was what their obstetrics and gynecology textbook said about women. The book stated that the feminine core is narcissism, masochism, and passivity. I was interested, and I got graduate students to do a little content analysis of gynecology textbooks with reference to what they said about women and sexuality. After all, gynecologists consider themselves, and are considered to be, experts in this area. We were rather appalled to find how very traditional and stereotyped the views expressed were. And these books are used to train people who do counseling!

Also, I wonder if there is anything that can be done to encourage more women not only to go to medical school, but also to go into obstetrics and gynecology, which has a very low percentage of women.

Dr. Long: I think the book the young lady is referring to is a classic or near-classic by Helene Deutsch, a Freudian psychiatrist who published a two-volume work on the psychology of women in 1944 and 1945. Helene Deutsch says that the feminine core was exactly as you have stated. As a gynecologist, I will not begin to comment on whether that is valid or invalid, or true or false. I just want to put it in its proper perspective. Some people believe it, and some people don't.

Comment: Dr. Masters, you brought up in your talk the problem that you feel exists now and that you say you view with dismay: that there are many people teaching "human sexuality" who are unprepared to teach. The other thing you talked about and placed a great deal of stress upon was communication. I wonder if people as perceptive as you seem to be must have, first of all, not been aware that there was going to be a tremendous demand for the type of material and information that you were presenting to the American public. That you were totally unprepared to meet this tremendous demand is a dismay to me. Second, how do you intend to communicate with those of us who perhaps are willing to help you with what you seem to have produced for us? I think you've done remarkable work, but now you leave us in a bind. You have opened, if you will, Pandora's box.

Dr. Masters: What I hoped I was warning you against was the corner treatment centers. There's a heck of a difference between teaching human sexuality and trying to treat as many cases of sexual dysfunction as you can in a corner treatment center. Let me give you an example. We're not just whistling in the dark here because so many places throughout the country use our names in advertisements. We've had a few of these places checked. On the West Coast, there's a lovely place that advertises in all the newspapers and periodicals that they are using our treatment. The man has just recently gotten out of jail. The females are members of a time-honored profession, but there's no professional in the group at all. It is this type of thing that I am dismayed with. The dissemination of information is a horse of a different color.

Comment: Well, what do you suggest we do about it?

Dr. Masters: There's no way in the world that we can control exactly what I was talking about, at this stage of the game, and under the current laws in the various states, in terms of practice. What I was suggesting was that we have meetings at a national level of representatives of medicine, theology, and the behavioral sciences. We should establish some neat, satisfactory code, and then insist that it be adopted. I'm not suggesting that I have the answer at all; I'm only suggesting, as we have been screaming for the last five years, that the public is going to demand adequate treatment. Where it is going to come from, I don't have the vaguest idea.

Dr. Long: I would just like to say that there has been very little recognition in the medical schools of the need for the sort of education Dr. Masters and Ms. Johnson are discussing. They are pioneers.

There were 82 medical schools in 1961; only three had courses of medical education in human sexuality. Today, there are 112 medical schools, and over 100 of them have courses in human sexuality. The demand brought about by the research that these wonderful people and others have done is being met. There will be a transitional period in which we can't begin to meet the public demand, but in time we will have a whole host of people — family practitioners, internists, OB-gyne men, and others who will have had this training in medical school and as residents.

Comment: I am a doctor and I have a comment to make on the use of the terms human sexuality in the title of this session. It seems to me to be a talk on couple enrichment, which I think is beautiful. I have nothing against one-to-one, heterosexual, long-commitment relationships, but there are millions of people who are not in love with an available sex partner. I also think that some of the teaching in the medical schools is inadequate still, and if it's according to the new American Medical Association book on human sexuality, I'm afraid it's full of bias. We're still learning about all kinds of life styles other than that of the married couple only from patients who are troubled and who seek help. Most psychiatrists, psychologists, and marriage counselors do not feel an obligation to study the life styles of people who are not sick, and they seem to write books only from data on sick patients.

Mr. Kupcinet: Does that bring forth any response?

Dr. Masters: I think she said it all, and I agree with her.

Mr. Kupcinet: How about you, Virginia, do you agree with her too?

Ms. Johnson: Portions of it, of course. We don't deal with "sick" patients, so I can't personally agree on that score. Ours is the study of natural sexual responsivity, and we recognize it and honor it in any form.

Part Five

Societal Values and
Value Change

Chapter 11

Societal Values: Impact on the American Scene

Harvey Wheeler*

We are talking about those people alive today who are in their 30s 40s and 50s. We know about these people because we are a part of them. With them, we have known nothing in our lifetimes but war, depression, violence and, lately, genocide, corruption on an enormous scale, a loss of national innocence, and a loss of international esteem. In short, this is the group that has experienced a stupendous change in values. And the changes have only just started. There is more to come.

VALUES AND VALUE CHANGE

Value changes can be said to arise from two basically different sources. The first we might call spiritual or ideational sources. One example would be changes in consciousness as described by Charles Reich in *The Greening of America*. Another example would be changes in religious ideology, spreading over our country today, such as the waves of fundamentalism and oriental philosophy that are changing our religious and spiritual conceptions. That is not the kind of value change I'm going to talk about.

The other kind of value change always goes along with the spiritual and ideational changes — sometimes reinforcing them, sometimes following them, sometimes preceding them, but always a part of them. These are the institutional sources of value changes, and by that I mean to include technology and science.

We are now living through a scientific revolution. When we speak of scientific revolution in our time, we have in mind certain very catastrophic, dominant, spectacular innovations. We think of the atomic bomb, and we think of the computer, and we think of what we now call the biological revolution.

*Harvey Wheeler, PhD, has been a senior fellow of the Center for the Study of Democratic Institutions, Santa Barbara, California, since 1960. Before that, he was a professor of political science at Johns Hopkins and Washington and Lee Universities.

When we compare these scientific innovations with the innovations of the late 19th century — that great era of inventions — we realize that there is a fundamental difference between recent innovations and those that made America great. McCormick, Edison, and Ford — those inventor-engineers and quasi-scientists — made their contributions largely in areas that expanded and extended the capacities of the human body. The innovations that are characteristic of today's scientific revolution are not of that sort at all. They are not extensions of human capacity or body parts. when we talk about the atomic bomb, we are talking about energy in general; when we talk about the computer, we are talking about thought in general; and when we talk about the biological revolution, we are talking about life in general.

One of the things that strikes us about the scientific innovations of our day is that finding a mass market for them is entirely different from finding a mass market for a reaper, a sewing machine, or an automobile. Those were innovations that every individual could use immediately, whereas all of our latest innovations come to us in a remote way and affect the entire web of our life relationships. Indeed, to use them, or exploit them, or benefit from them very likely would require a large system change in society. The system changes that are implicit in these innovations have not really arrived yet. If there is anything to this proposition, there are massive changes in store for us. Up until about 1920, whether we were Marxist or not, we had an idea that capital was pretty important. It might not go exactly the way Marx said, but if it didn't go that way, it went the way that Andrew Carnegie said, which was just about the same thing, except that he was in favor of capital and Marx was against it. In any case, it was a capitalist society, and if you owned all the capital in the society, there was little doubt that you could control society. You could not only control the society, but also more or less say what was going to happen in the future.

I'm not saying that capital is unimportant today, but I am saying that the role of innovation is threatening and almost displacing the role of capital. For example, if you and I here tonight could control the entire United States' endeavor in scientific research over the next five or six years, we could decide what science was going to be produced. By that decision, we would also be establishing the overall social, cultural, and intellectual framework within which future changes and developments would be taking place. Control over the flow of innovation now comes to rival control over the flow of capital. This, of course, has enormous implications for value change.

All of our many values have been related to capital and the capitalist way. We speak of the Protestant ethic as central in the American way of life, and that, of course, is directly related to the industrial way of life, the capital way of life. If indeed it does come to pass that there is a transition away from the Protestant ethic to a different kind of ethic, there are some difficulties following in its wake.

IMPLICATIONS OF THE COMPUTER

Employing computers in the chain of functions that are sometimes called decision routines in a large-scale organization has the effect of putting equipment between man and the decisions he makes. Let us use as an example the man who, it is said, computers would like to emulate — Robert McNamara. He was an executive at Ford Motor Company, former U. S. Secretary of Defense, and now head of the World Bank. Maybe he is why the monetary situation has gotten worse, all of a sudden. I never thought of that before. First he built the Edsel. Then he was in the Pentagon when the TFX was built — that plane that practically never flew anywhere. Now, we've got the dollar crisis.

That is probably giving him too much credit, but nonetheless I want to point out to you one thing that happens in a decision-making process that is characterized by highly computerized procedures. The end result may not add up to a decision at all. Individual decisions may be made here and there throughout a huge organization, and they may not come out collectively as a real, live, rational, integrated decision. An example is my favorite automobile, the Edsel, a kind of nonautomobile. It had wheels, and a motor, and all that sort of thing, but it was built by computers. The company went out and did all this market research, and fed the information into the computer. The machine that came out at the other end of the line was a noncar.

Something like that happened with the airplane that has killed so many of our flyers, the TFX. I feel the same way about the decision that we got into in Vietnam. One thing that emerges dramatically from the Pentagon papers is that the movement into the war was based on a nondecision. There were all these pieces. You can study what this department said and that department said, and nobody wanted war, but that's where it all ended up.

I'm suggesting that computerized decision-making produces non-decisions. It is possible to have a huge organization acting on a decision of this sort that no single person in the organization is in favor of and yet everyone has participated in producing. Everyone may be against it, and yet they are all committed to carrying it out.

The second aspect of a computerized operation has to do with a difference in the basis on which decisions are made. As you may well know, computerized decision-making is done mainly by mathematical routines, and one of the most predominant mathematical routines for programming decisions is game theory. A program applying game theory relies on a minimax principle; that is, when we want to evaluate the various alternatives open to us, we say that we will choose that decision that minimizes our maximum possible losses. This is a statistical concept, and you can't deal with it any other way but statistically.

Admiral Radford, who was kind of a computerized admiral, was once asked by *Time* magazine what were some of the greatest decisions he ever made. He sat back on his haunches and said, well, decision-making is something that I very seldom do. I make a decision only when the answer to a problem is not implicit in the data. Now, contrast this with another admiral, Admiral Farragut, who said, "Damn the torpedoes, full speed ahead." It's the difference between minimax decision-making today and the seat-of-your pants decision-making practiced by men like Henry Ford in earlier days.

We all grew up in an era when symbols were meaningful. Even if we didn't understand them personally, they meant something to someone. The symbolic environment that we grew up in was the so-called dollar-sign environment that was supposed to be so characteristic of the American way of life. All the great novelists, like Sinclair Lewis, made their reputations by calling our attention to this dollar symbol standing before our dollar-glazed eyes. I would like to suggest that, as the computer era matures, while there will still be dollars around and people around to celebrate our commitment to them, they will be joined in the symbolic framework by computer symbols.

Almost all of you, I think, have heard of the book, *The Limits to Growth*, the Club of Rome report. Possibly you know that the report makes use of a computer program model of the world based on five variables that are alleged to describe an ecological whole. Then there is a number of simultaneous equations that are worked out. When you run all this through the computer, you come out with the prediction of death, destruction, and catastrophe by the year 2000. All I ask you to do is to look at the first appendix to this book, and you will see the future, because it consists of the formulae that were used to derive the model that produced the ideas in *The Limits to Growth*. Here are the computer symbols that illustrate the kind of symbolic world most of us will be living in in the future.

It is not just people like the MIT mathematicians and engineers who produced the Club of Rome Report who are making use of computerized data. You can't build a city from scratch these days. You first find a computer man, who runs your data through a series of models, something like the Club of Rome formulae, which produces a program in the form of a print-out. From there, you go on and build a city.

I'm not against this use of the computer, you understand; there is no point in fighting it. But we are all going to change our symbolic environment. We used to say the dollar was God. I suppose we will come to a new kind of Pythagoreanism. Pythagoreans viewed the universe as being made up of numbers that had religious significance. I feel that Pythagorean symbolic environment or a number symbol realm of discourse will be increasingly characteristic of the environment we live in.

OPERANT CONDITIONING AND B. F. SKINNER

First, I'll characterize operant conditioning very briefly. It is related to the behaviorism of the past that most of us are familiar with — you know, Pavlov and his dog that salivated when a bell was rung. Pavlovian behaviorism is based on a stimulus-response model. It is like a classical, mechanical model. If you put force in one side, you get work out the other, or stimulus and response.

While not denying that this can happen in behavior, especially with regard to autonomic nervous system behavior or responses such as the knee jerk, Skinner concentrates on what happens after behavior occurs, responses to behavior coming from the environment. Specifically, he focuses on the ways in which behavior is reinforced or not by either reward or punishment after the fact. So it is a post hoc kind of conditioning that Skinner is talking about.

Skinner concludes from his studies that rewards coming after the behavior are much more powerful behavior-modifiers than punishment. If Skinner's thesis is true, and there is a certain amount of evidence for it, and if this idea of behavior has as much effect as its predecessor, then we are in for some drastic value changes.

The early behaviorism we are talking about here is that of John Locke, Jeremy Bentham, and John Stewart Mill, and the pleasure-pain psychologists — the kind we learned about when we came through college. For example, if you wanted to write a criminal law properly, you figured out just exactly how much pleasure a fellow might get from doing this thing you didn't want him to do, which therefore you called a crime, and you counterbalanced that with just a little bit more pain in the law to discourage him from committing the crime. So a man goes through life in a criminal-law type society, a punitive society. Almost all our legislation today is of this kind, especially our criminal law; we penalize the behavior that we don't want. We try to penalize it out of existence, the punitive approach.

Now, if the Skinnerians are correct, punishment is not only a less effective way of shaping behavior, it is also positively harmful. In the past, a punitive approach might have been essential to the preservation of the species, to the development of man, and to his survival. But when societies get more complex and more intertwined, the punishment approach and its elaborations tend to produce a punitive society and punitive people. Punishment begets punishment.

I was visiting an institution for mental patients run entirely along operant conditioning lines. There were a lot of placards around on the walls. As I walked in the door, one came right out at me. In big, block letters it said, "Hurt people, hurt people." That was the placard. I looked at it, and I thought, "My God, what's this?" until I realized that you can read it, "Hurt people hurt people." You have to break that chain of punishment somewhere, say the operant conditioning people, so you move into it by trying to help people not hurt themselves so much, reduce the internal hurting, and thereby reduce the amount of hurt and punishment in society.

Consider a society that did not use punitive measures in its criminal law, but instead used reinforcers for the behaviors that it wanted to elicit. It is a startling thing, but there are many, many indications that it is going to work out in places where it is now being used. It is being used very effectively in business organizations. Instead of punitive regulations, businesses and governmental organizations are offering positive reinforcements.

Operant conditioning will have a great impact on our concept of the individualistic, autonomous personality. We will have to mount a very serious investigation of this kind of thing before introducing it into society. It is all right to introduce it in some business organizations because you can always change it. But before it is introduced as part of the national system, it certainly needs considerable evaluation, or technological assessment.

THE BIOLOGICAL REVOLUTION

The geneticists now tell us with some degree of confidence that within the next 10, 15, maybe 20 years, man's life span is going to be stretched out by perhaps as much as 20 years. Let's assume that's the case. There are a lot of ifs involved, and I could go into the technical details, the molecular biology, of the current theories if anybody wants to, but for the sake of argument let's accept it as true. Let's say that tomorrow morning's papers announce that a longevity pill is now available at the nearest drugstore or from a physician, and that it is going to give you 20 years more life. By the way, another thing the gerontologists tell us is that it won't just add 20 years of senescence. We won't have 20 years added on after age 80 so that you just have 20 more years in the condition you are in at 80, 85, or 90. No, the idea is to add that 20 years to the middle years, or what I like to refer to, in talking of such people, as the prime-time society.

Let us say we are talking about someone age 45 who is going to have the same amount of vigor he has now for the next 35 years. What is the effect, emotionally and psychologically, of that first increment you get? You see, it isn't just 20 more years, because the emotional meaning of it is that it almost doubles the time you have in the full power of life.

What I am getting at is that the first impact is more than just the sheer numbers you are adding. The emotional impact stretches out your life, your effective power, for considerably longer. So, what are you going to think? Is this 20 years brought to you by the same science that gave you chlorophyll and deodorants? Is it 20 years and no more? Not on your life, brother. That same outfit is going to come back before my 20 years is up, because they are working in the laboratories night and day and they want those Nobel prizes, and they are going to offer me another 20 years before these are used up.

We have all grown up with conceptions and expectations of mortality, of death — imminent death — especially, in the middle years. Paul Tillich defines this anxiety as characteristic of the middle years — the rational confrontation of man with the conception of his mortality, his imminent end. Tillich goes on to identify almost all religious feeling with this confrontation, this anxiety.

What is going to happen to people with the gift of 20 years? Will it not be the case that people will begin to reverse their expectations? Instead of expecting and anticipating death, will not their expectations shift to infinite prolongation of life? Even though the first announcement only gave you 20 years, wouldn't you expect, aha, there is going to be more and more, life without end, right? So, what do you do with a society of immortals? It really doesn't make any difference whether they really are immortal, in actual biological fact, because some people are going to get run over, you know, and that is going to be horrible. Like, my God, I just took my pill, and the guy ran over me — zonk! That is going to be horrible. It is bad enough to die now, but when it's all eternity going down the drain. . . . Would not your expectation be of immortality rather than mortality, and if that were the case, can you see how value systems would be affected?

Let's take a moral issue related to that. One of the things we know is that some people can die from taking common medications such as aspirin. With almost any drug, a certain proportion of people who take it have a reaction opposite to that usually shown. Some people, when you give them a tranquilizer, get hyperactive, and when you give them an energizer, go to sleep. So, suppose the immortality pill is deadly to a certain percentage of the people.

Imagine the social and political implications of a pill that may have great benefits for many people and a lethal effect on others? How is a society going to handle that kind of problem? We have great difficulty handling our science-related problems today, but these biological breakthroughs are going to bring problems that are much more serious.

The situation hypothesized before would, in effect, create a strange two-class society. Some people would refuse to take the immortality pill on principle. Add to those the ones on whom the pill would have adverse effects and you might have a proportion of society as high as 20% or 30%. Seventy percent of the people would be immortals and 30% would be mortals. Now, that is a real class society, and it would have enormously severe implications.

What about murder in such a society? Suppose you have 20 more years — not full immortality, but just the 20 years they are telling us about in today's papers. Murder would become a much more horrendous event. In fact, murder might become a major cause of death, along with accidents. Time would become of great value, and you would have to go around with bodyguards all the time. The bodyguard business would probably be a big industry in a society of immortals.

Well, while I have been joshing with some of these examples, I think you realize that I am very serious about these problems and issues. The main thing is that they portend a tremendous upheaval of morals and values — a building up for an ethical earthquake in society. All Western ethics have been built upon a notion of man reacting to a basically immutable universe, whereas what we are talking about now is a completely mutable, plastic universe — something for which there has been no ethical system devised. The new ethics will be one of the most challenging inventions confronting us in the middle years and the years beyond.

Chapter 12

The Human Agenda

Roderic Gorney*

Let us place the problems of the middle years in the context of how we can contribute to the survival of the endangered human species. What I'm going to tell you is a condensation of an outline of an abstract of a précis of *The Human Agenda*, which has been described as a "manual on how to be at home in the universe." To convey its premise, I'll have to touch on a wide variety of topics, including:

The implications of the present instant in human development
The evolution of values
The significance of cooperation
Instincts and aggression
The role of possible future abundance
The new biology
Happiness, and love, work, and play
Some conclusions

THE PRESENT INSTANT

In the evolution of man there is cause for realistic hope of human survival. Why is this the most marvelous moment of man in which to be alive? In this age of pollution, poverty, threats of nuclear war, racism, injustice, and so forth, for the first time in our 2 to 4 million years as a species, we also have the as-yet-unrealized possibility of having enough to go around so that all human lives could be fulfilled human lives. I don't mean only material things. I mean education, opportunity, love, imagination.

There are many people today, often very powerful people, who do not look upon this possibility happily. They are so terrorized at waking up, cast adrift in paradise without the map of scarcity to tell them what's good, what's bad, what's better or worse, who is superior and who is inferior, that they would rather press the button and atomize us all. Unconsciously, they are much more afraid that they will survive into this new era than that they will be exterminated.

---

*Roderic Gorney, MD, is a Los Angeles psychiatrist and psychoanalyst who also is a faculty member of the Department of Psychiatry at the UCLA School of Medicine and director of the department's new program on psychosocial adaptation and the future.

VALUES

Our societies are maintained and our cultures are transmitted from generation to generation in accordance with judgments that we call values — judgments about the worth of one thing relative to another. Values are the specific human means of adaptation. We don't develop wings or gills or specialized hooves. We maintain a generalized body plan, and we specialize our values and our social relationships to meet all contingencies. Values become woven into value systems.

In our country and others of the industrialized West, the nominal value system is the Puritan ethic. The Puritan ethic prizes hard work, thrift, frugality, chastity, respect for elders, submission to the will of God, and it is marvelously suited as an adaptation to conditions of scarcity. However, the Puritan ethic is maladaptive to conditions of increasing abundance. For example, thrift and frugality are fundamentally incompatible with a credit economy, and chastity seems to have been increasing in ir-relevance over the past 30 years.

Cooperation

New values for the era of abundance would have to be centered not just around preserving human life, but around cooperation for enrichment of human life. Cooperation is not a saintly human luxury. Cooperation is the fundamental law of all life. You may read renowned authors who disagree, but despite the self-serving distortions of Darwin by the "social Darwinists" who rationalize the status quo, life does not survive mainly by competition. Since life began, 3½ billion years ago, every species that has succeeded on this planet has done so by *cooperating with the other members of its species*. For example, one-celled animals and plants in the water (similar to the earliest species), grow better, feed faster, reproduce more abundantly if they are grouped close together than if they are far apart. The competition that we see throughout life on this planet is mainly *between* species. Yet many people tell us that the competition we see between human beings is matched all through plant and animal evolution, and even transmitted from them to man by genetic inheritance. That's just not so.

Man has lived most of his 2 to 4 million years on this planet in ac-cordance with the basic law of cooperation. Until civilization began 10,000 to 12,000 years ago, relationships between human beings, like those of most hunters and gatherers today, were cooperative and peaceful because they needed one another to survive. No great differences in material goods, power, or security developed between people of one group because they could not generate much wealth or carry large surpluses with them.

Their societies had a high degree of "social synergy," that is, their social arrangements were so organized that an individual could satisfy both his own needs and those of his group by the same act. If a man killed an antelope one day and his neighbor didn't, he shared the meat, so that his neighbor would be strong for the hunt the next day when he himself might be less fortunate and in turn need help. There was no advantage to anyone in having poor neighbors.

Exploitation and Competition

With the beginning of civilization and the development of techniques of farming and herding, people for the first time could settle down in fixed agricultural communities. For the first time in human experience, ownership of land became important because plant and animal foods that previously had to be hunted in the wild could be raised right outside the door. Now it became possible to store reserves of food, fuel, clothing, and other riches on one's land for greater security against the elements in time of drought, flood, or other catastrophe.

Marked differences in wealth developed between rich and poor classes. Now — for the first time — it became valuable for one to have poor neighbors who could be hired to work for low wages to further enrich oneself. And so it became useful to prevent others from owning land of their own. As a result, advancing human societies thereafter often developed low social synergy. For example, a man could satisfy the group's need for cheap labor by selling himself into slavery, but he could *not* satisfy his own needs by the same act.

Out of this sort of circumstance arose, over thousands of years, the enormous exploitativeness and competitiveness between human beings that we observe today. But these behaviors have been *learned* by our species only in the last ½% of our existence on earth. Because these behaviors are not instinctual, they can be unlearned.

INSTINCTS AND AGGRESSION

People ask, "Isn't it innate to have an aggressive, violent drive, like the instincts of sex and acquisitiveness?" The answer is easy: "No." No matter what you hear, human beings do not have any such instincts. In fact, humans do not have instincts at all, in the sense that lower animals do, that is, inherited, spontaneous behavior patterns with built-in action patterns for carrying out impulses.

Someone once said correctly, "A man is an animal who has lost all of his instincts and none of his impulses." Unlike certain birds and fish, we primates do not have pre-programmed knowledge directing our reactions to our impulses, such as those connected with the drives of hunger, thirst, sex, and so on. The best evidence of this is the rhesus monkey, a distant relative of ours fairly far down the primate scale, that will never learn to copulate unless it has had the proper *social learning experiences*. That seems to be true of all the "higher" primates — monkeys, apes, and humans. For them, sexual behavior is not much of an instinct. If you want to see bewilderment in the absence of instinctual knowledge, watch a sexually mature and interested but inexperienced rhesus monkey male and female when they are brought together, and see how they bumble around trying to figure out what to do about their impulses.

Instincts do exist among the "lower" animals. For example, the male cichlid fighting fish is impelled every 45 minutes or so by a spontaneous drive and built-in action pattern to attack another male if one is around, or to attack his own mate, a stone, or the empty corner of his aquarium if he is alone. Aggressive and reproductive instincts are also found in some birds, but they fade out in the "lower" mammals, and they have disappeared in the primates.

As Ashley Montagu says, "Human nature is what man learns." Montagu has also pointed out that Konrad Lorenz and others have taken their observations from fish and birds and extrapolated them to man without sufficient study of intervening animals, something the "dean of ethology" (Lorenz) would not do even between two related species of geese. As Montagu succinctly stated, "Observations from fish and birds are strictly for them."

Now, we must not be naive. Human beings are born with a physiological mechanism which, with *proper training* and *provocation*, can respond with violence. If somebody steps on your corn while you are riding one of Chicago's buses, you may feel like attacking him, or you may even do it. But you don't feel or behave that way every 45 minutes, regardless of what is happening to you, like the cichlid fighting fish. The response must be evoked from you or provoked.

As a human being, you can decide whether or not to act on an urge. It's a great cop-out to say, "Well, it's too bad we were born violent, but our animal ancestors are to blame." That way we never have to feel responsible for or pay attention to the social injustices that lead to the aggression and violence that plague us today. The immense popularity of books that trumpet this cop-out, such as some of those of Lorenz, Ardrey, Morris, and Storr, is based not only on their authors' talent for writing, but also on our need for a rationalization of vicious behavior.

FUTURE ABUNDANCE

Humankind has always been menaced primarily by scarcity, not by predators. For that reason, all our basic activities — our love, our work, and our play — have been in bondage to the elemental problem of surviving amid scarcity. Civilization, with its technologies for abundance, increasingly has given us the tools with which to exterminate scarcity, and we stand right now on the threshold of the possibility of having enough to go around for everyone.

Therefore, *we could resume the cooperative values of the stone age that predominated before the onset of civilization, and simultaneously enjoy the benefits of the abundance we are potentially able to provide for everyone in the post-industrial era.* I'm sure you realize as I do that this constitutes a secluar possibility of the realization of a basic ethic of every great religion. We are held back from taking this crucial step not by technical incapacity, but by failure of character, imagination, and social organization.

This failure is optional. In *The Human Agenda*, I have sketched the possible dimensions of this abundance. By the year 2000, our species could arrange for every family of four then alive to have an annual income of $7,500 1965 US dollars. While this is not a lot by US standards, it is munificent by those of Africa, Asia, and South America. It is twice the standard of living currently enjoyed by the people of Ireland. Herman Kahn, who is not noted for rosy optimism, doubles my estimate. If those of us in this room were to use our middle years assiduously promulgating such understanding, we could spread it widely, and those to whom we talk could immeasurably increase its effect.

The human species is unique in that it largely retains imaginative, spontaneous, and creative capabilities all through life, whereas other animals lose their spontaneity, gaiety, and imaginativeness when they grow old. I'm reminded of a situation in which I learned a great deal from a 94-year-old Danish sea carpenter who was far beyond middle age, but who helped a young man just entering psychiatric practice to deal with a very complex situation. The 26-year-old daughter of a hard-working Italian immigrant family was referred to me by the family doctor. He described this daughter as exceptionally pretty, sweet, submissive, diligent, and self-sacrificing. She suffered from many physical troubles that this doctor assumed were due to her emotional trouble, and he wanted me to find out what that was and help her. When I opened the waiting-room door, I was overpowered by a cascade of descriptions of her problem in Italian from a roomful of relatives. There were about eight relatives and this 94-year-old Danish family retainer.

Listening quietly in the corner, the retired sea carpenter who had been with the family as a handyman since his retirement from the sea long ago, paid attention but said nothing. From the babble I caught only a few words, such as fainting spells, paralyzed arms, swollen belly, numbness below the waist — the sort of complaints that are common in the condition called hysteria. Sensing my bewilderment after a moment, the old man silenced all of these relatives with a gesture and eloquently gave me the diagnosis. "Doctor, these people don't understand this girl at all. The trouble with her is very simple. She has too much of what the tomcats fight over, and too much upbringing to make the most of it." I have never forgotten the lesson I learned then, that in one's youth it's possible to learn a great deal that you can transmit to others in your old age. I offer those of you who are not happy about middle age this solace for the gradual decline of certain other opportunities as we grow older.

THE NEW BIOLOGY

One aspect of abundance that I try to make people aware of is the new biology, because people need to know so that they can help influence what's done about it. There are new controls over the process of gestation that are available right now today, but which have not been used yet in human beings. They have been used in other animals, and what can be done in one mammal is just a matter of a little technique to do in another. For example, a certain strain of English sheep was needed in Africa a couple of years ago. The problem of introducing the strain was very easily solved by biologists, who transplanted the embryos from the ewes in England to the uteri of rabbits. Imagine that — you can even transplant an embryo from one species to another! The rabbits, being small, were conveniently flown to Africa and unloaded. The embryos were promptly extracted from the rabbits, transplanted into the wombs of the African sheep who thereupon gave birth 5½ months later to their aristocratic English cousins to whom they had no genetic relationship.

Foster wombing will create a lot of outrage when doctors first attempt it with human beings, but one of these days there will be a young mother dying of leukemia who would like to save her unborn child for her husband who will survive her. At that point, I think we're likely to find an accommodation of old taboos to new realities, because we all want to save life. The doctor someplace in this world, will transplant that embryo into the womb of the woman's sister, who has offered to gestate the child for her doomed sibling. If the baby is born healthy there is likely to be little protest.

Then, a young actress will go to that doctor, and say, "Oh, doctor, it's very inconvenient for me to be eight-months pregnant next summer when I'm making a film in Rome. Won't you please transplant this embryo from me to my secretary who has volunteered." Obviously, there are all kinds of moral and legal implications here that were not present in the earlier example. Suppose the secretary gets tired of the pregnancy and wants to give the embryo back three months later. Or suppose she grows attached to the child and refuses to return it after delivery. Whose child is it? And is it justified to subject two women and an unborn child to the risks of surgery when there is no medical need to do so? Before leaving this tangle, I must tell you the remark of Norman Corwin, renowned radio and television writer: "If foster wombing becomes a profession, at least we can look forward for the first time to a labor union worthy of the name."

Some months ago, four men came to see me in my office requesting that embryo babies be transplanted into *their* abdomens because they wanted to be mothers. Don't frown too hard; it makes wrinkles in middle age! In *The Human Agenda* I wrote about this possibility abstractly as a prospect for the *future*. Here was a delegation demanding it as a concrete reality in the present.

What is the basis for such an idea? Under certain conditions it is quite possible for male mammary glands to secrete milk. There are reports in past centuries of Chinese men functioning as wet nurses. It is also potentially quite possible to prepare a male body so that it can receive and gestate an unborn baby, in either a transplanted uterus or some other convenient spot in the abdomen. Eventually someone will arrange such a transplant and nine months later a baby will be delivered by Caesarean section into the loving arms of a nursing father! Please notice, I am not recommending any of this; I am simply reporting to you what is being learned scientifically and some repercussions in Los Angeles.

Two of the delegation were transvestites, or men who like to wear women's clothes. Incidentally, both of them were married and had fathered children. The third was a homosexual man who said he was married to another man. The fourth was a transexual man, or a person who has grown up feeling that he is really the opposite sex. This man, like Christine Jorgenson, had had the surgery that transformed him legally into a woman, entitled to marry a man, which he had done five years ago. He said, "If I am accepted as a woman sexually, socially, and legally, why should I be denied the right to have a child? I demand an embryo transplant." The homosexual man then spoke up. "About 10% of the population is homosexual, of which a large proportion would like to have babies of their own. Why should we be denied the opportunity?" Finally, a transvestite declared, "I'm a very good father. Now, I'd like to bear a child myself." I explained lamely that, as a psychiatrist, I had nothing to do with surgery. They set off to see a gynecologist, leaving me with my thoughts, as I must leave you with yours. Again, I'm not recommending embryo transplantation, but I am suggesting that we should start now to consider the social implications of abundant new biological possibilities before they are realized.

HAPPINESS AND LOVE, WORK, AND PLAY

Thomas Jefferson's phrase, "the pursuit of happiness," was a great step forward in the description of an essential human goal. But, as Albert Einstein once commented, "Happiness is for pigs." He meant that happiness is always a by-product of human relationships or accomplishments, and therefore cannot be achieved, even under conditions of abundance, by direct pursuit.

Human relationships and accomplishments are all created in the course of our three fundamental human activities: love, work, and play. All three have always been in bondage to just staying alive and so have become, in the era of scarcity, the routes only to restricted satisfactions and happiness. Love has always been shackled mainly to generating and nurturing children, and work to producing and obtaining goods and services needed to sustain us. Play, unfortunately, has always functioned mainly as an escape from the misery we encounter in our love and work! In the future we could emancipate all three to serve as means to enrich life's adventure, and thus restore the cooperative values of the stone age amid the post-industrial era's abundance.

Instead of this thrilling prospect, what are we offered by those who entice us to direct pursuit of happiness? One source of this so-called happiness is mass entertainment, an area of human endeavor little studied for its effects on adults, although it reaches virtually everyone. Seventy-five million people a night watch entertainment television, 40 million a week watch entertainment motion pictures, and 100 million more read entertainment magazines, newspapers, and books.

Consider, for example, *Playboy* magazine and other enterprises, at home here in Chicago. Let us look together at their effect upon human happiness — and let us form a bodyguard for me as I leave the auditorium. *Playboy* is supposedly the knight errant on behalf of the sensuality of sex which, it hopes, it's going to liberate from all the Puritanical chains. A new dogma, as I see it, is substituted for the old. Sex is good, let it rip. Bring on the "bunny."

What are we to feel toward a bunny? Literally, a bunny is an infantile rabbit valued by human beings for its cuteness and the fact that eventually it will be edible. Affection, and the minor sensuality that goes with stroking a bunny, are about all you can expect. However, not even the petting is returned, and any sort of mutual relationship with a bunny is unthinkable by definition. Later, when the bunny has matured, the best that one can say for a bunny is that, with minimal protest on its part, it can be eaten, erasing its identity as it is nutritionally incorporated into one's own identity. Come to think of it, that's not a bad description of many marriages. Maybe the bunny theory of marriage ought to be published. Or maybe it should be called the "Twinkie theory of marriage."

At least, you can stroke a real bunny. In *Playboy's* peekaboo paradise we are not even permitted to touch. So, apparently what we are expected to experience toward the pretty, youthful, but undistinctive creatures called "bunny" whose futures, incidentally, end at 25, is a strange amalgam of clean lust and parental protectiveness. This assures that our sexual sensuality regresses to a sort of gluttonous infantile voyeurism as we look through the *Playboy* keyholes. Sometimes I am asked, "After all, hasn't *Playboy* done a great deal to increase happiness by freeing sex from Victorian shackles through unclothing the girl next door instead of a prostitute?" I have to answer, "No," for there is no true acceptance of sex here either. Instead sex has been reduced either to that bland American institution called good, clean fun, or to the spirit of naughtiness found at a teen-age pajama party. The fresh young girls in the centerfolds, I am told, go to bed with the same passionless enthusiasm with which they eat pizza. And as any man of experience will tell you — I see there are other graybeards here today — such young women are not yet fully awakened sexually, no matter how long ago the alarm went off.

If the sexual revolution, which is supposed to emancipate us middle-aged people as well as the youth, must depend upon Hefner's kindergarten, then God help it — if He isn't dead.

Looking at the rest of love today, how many people maintain marriages, despite having lost interest in one another, just "for the sake of the children?" With respect to work, how many of us know work we would do well if we did not need a paycheck? And turning to play, how many of us can engage in play for the delight in the activity *itself*, rather than the

138

spurious compensation for love and work frustrations of "beating" someone at a game? Very few.

This is the human present, but it is not a truly humane future. I propose that we employ abundance to emancipate love, work, and play from sheer preservation of life and let them come instead to *enrich* life so that the next generation of young people, by the time they reach middle age, will have a zestful sense of discovery moving into the next century, and not the gloomy, hopeless despair endured by so many people today who don't grasp the new possibilities.

SOME CONCLUSIONS

In this new world of abundance, including the abundance of rapid change, we have to learn to live with uncertainty. Paradoxically, as we eliminate the certainty of scarcity, we must come to live with *uncertainty* about everything else that once seemed sure, and we must learn not to seize upon new dogmas to persuade ourselves once again that we do know everything. I know people who switch every month, expecting magic each time, from astrology to macrobiotic diet to psychoanalysis to nude marathons to politics to Zen and back, grasping at assurances that they now know the truth for all time. Of course no doctrine, no school or technique, gives you the perfect truth eternal. And we must recognize that we may not be wise enough to use this new possibility of abundance, to make human lives better than they were in the past, unless we use our primate flexibility and try very hard.

We must remember, to paraphrase Oscar Wilde, that "there is no man in the world so pitiful as one who does not get his heart's desire unless it is one who does." Think about that. . . . I see a lot of people who've gotten their heart's desire, who already enjoy a kind of abundance. What they are doing in a psychiatrist's office puzzles them. But it should not puzzle us. As we have seen, abundance and direct pursuit of happiness does not *assure* happiness. If we now simply reverse the emphasis of the Puritan ethic so that we pursue play, sensuality, and happiness while squelching hard work, thrift, and frugality, we face as dismal a fate as before. We are in danger of becoming a species that has learned to satisfy all its wishes without ever having learned to wish for all its satisfactions. I mean by that that love, work, and play must continue as the fundamentals of human well-being in the world of abundance, even though they must serve the purpose of enriching rather than preserving life. People who don't continue to love, work, and play are apt to be miserable in the changed world of tomorrow.

Let me close by illustrating the basic human situation as I see it. A baby who is racked with hunger pains will suckle vigorously. If, at the same time, he is exhausted, he may fall asleep before his stomach is full and so stop suckling, only to be awakened again by the next wave of hunger pains. Whether to eat or to sleep first is not a dilemma imposed upon him by pollution, racism, poverty, chauvinism, Republicanism, or any other external factor. It is a conflict built into his biology. Although later on most conflict is not biological, throughout most of our lives we will be subject to a great deal of it. We have to learn that this is a condition of man, learn to put up with it, and not to expect perfect relief. Maturity depends upon unflinchingly facing the choices we have and the sacrifices we must make that are implicit in any choice we make. That includes dealing with people as separate creatures and not trying to devour them in one way or another.

In the words of Dr. Henry A. Murray of Harvard, "If I have said anything for which I should be sorry, I am willing to be forgiven."

The human situation includes the realistic grounds for hope, hope that human beings can move fast enough to ward off threats to our survival. Some people might call such hope optimistic. However, I am not an optimist. An optimist is often a compulsively cheery person who is happy despite the facts. Sometimes I wake up as blue as anyone in this audience. It is the facts that then cheer me up.

To prove I am not an optimist but a hopeful realist, consider this time perspective: Before our species was invented, there were two and a half million generations of apes on this planet. They remained stooped, languageless, and static throughout their history. Out of one of their lines developed our ancestors — early humans. How many generations ago do you think that was? Only 80,000.

Now nothing much happened to change human life until people learned to tame fire. That was barely 20,000 generations ago. How many generations have lived since the beginning of civilization? Five hundred! Every aspect of civilization has been achieved by the last 500 generations. Recorded history is only 250 generations old. The Golden Age of Greece came 100 generations ago, and Jesus lived and died shortly after. The entire scientific revolution is encompassed by the last 20 generations. The scientific study of the mind is only three generations old. And the possibility of universal basic human abundance was articulated only three quarters of one generation ago by Buckminster Fuller.

Now with this kind of time perspective, the only posture for a human being is one of considered hope. In fact, I take great encouragement from the speed with which our innovations have brought us to the threshold of fulfillment — or to the edge of doom.

Appendix

Since the Quality of Life series is designed to increase the level of public awareness and the recognition that life is a continuum, we are including in this volume three of the key papers presented at Congress I concentrating on improving the quality of life of mothers, infants, children and youth. The habits, practices, life styles and moral values developed and cultivated during any one phase of life's continuum will have their impact on the quality of life as one grows older.

A.

The Purpose of Congress I

*The quality of life of a baby
begins with the birth of its parents.*

The Congress on the Quality of Life, 1972 concentrated on maternal and child health from conception through adolescence within a social, environmental, and educational frame of reference. The meeting was sponsored by the American Medical Association in cooperation with other professional, voluntary, and governmental agencies.

This landmark meeting was intended to increase the level of public awareness of the importance of all children and to initiate a plan for inter-group action on behalf of children at the national, regional, state, and local levels. In other words, we hope to make children the nation's highest priority because they *are* the future nation.

The quality of life at all age levels has been deteriorating. Since a single Congress cannot address itself to the total life span, this Congress focused on the early years as the period during which the stage is set for much that follows throughout life. The foundation years are crucial if primary prevention is to be realized on a meaningful scale.

Prevention is much more than immunization and screening tests. It involves assuring the orderly growth and development of children. This orderly development depends upon the relationship of the physical, social, and educational environments. The cost of maintaining blighted individuals in society is seldom considered in relation to the cost of prevention. Prevention protects the human potential and provides better return for financial expenditure.

Mentally and physically handicapping conditions that limit individual potential are occurring at an ever increasing rate. The root causes of many of these conditions are found in circumstances surrounding pregnancy, childhood, and adolescence. Examples of such conditions are malnutrition, mental retardation, cerebral palsy, emotional disturbances, learning disabilities, alcoholism, unplanned pregnancy, drug abuse, and aggressive behavior.

These are complex problems that cannot be prevented or managed by physicians alone — nor by any other professional discipline alone. Planned intergroup cooperation is essential for success in overcoming these problems.

The significant improvement in child care that has resulted from the several White House conferences, the efforts of the National Committee on Children and Youth, and the work of other national groups is note-worthy. Much more must be done to make what is known in health science available to *all* children. The existing programs often are fragmented and too narrow in scope, and fail to reach large numbers of children and youth in need — both affluent and poor. Of great importance also is the fact that children do not fare well in competition for program funds at any level of government.

Every community must be mobilized for action on behalf of our children. This will require *sustained* cooperative intergroup effort of the private and public sectors at the national, regional, state, and local levels. Business and industry have a big stake in this because it is the quality of people that determines the economic and political future of our country. An individual's worth to himself, his importance as a contributing member of society, his value as an employee, and his potential as a consumer are ultimately the function of his physical and mental well-being.

It was the aim of this Congress to plan ways of overcoming human blight that prevents children from being born healthy, developing properly, and reaching full potential.

The American Medical Association

B.

The Quality of Life
Today and Tomorrow

The concept of a "quality of life" may be as hazy as a concept of "love". Love is very difficult to define with the kind of accuracy demanded by those who seek to pin it down — to quantify something that is itself a quality. Adherents of any scientific discipline tend to panic when asked to investigate or deal with love. But almost everyone knows love is a reality — more of a reality than some scientific concepts that have been believed in and then disproved, concepts such as a flat geocentric world, phlogiston, caloric fluid, and the ether.

In the same way, quality of life is difficult to deal with, and yet we know there is something under that title that we can believe in. And we further know that there are conditions, methods, circumstances that can affect quality of life and that we can deal with in logical ways to effect changes in that quality.

Happiness is a root concept in the definition of quality of life, and happiness requires a mixture of hope, fulfillment, growth, and joyousness in an individual's existence. We are also certain, we can take as axiomatic, that the opposites of these elements — despair, frustration, stunting, and misery — are sure to prevent any meaningful quality of life in a given individual.

We further believe, or we wouldn't be here at this Congress, that certain actions by individuals and organizations can be taken, certain methods followed, that can improve the quality of life for someone or everyone (particularly those yet to be born), and that intelligent approaches will guide us to those actions and methods. The matter cannot be left to chance.

Many years ago the front page of the *Chicago Tribune* showed a cartoon by McCutcheon (the elder) titled "Two Aspects of Triumph." It was in two panels, the first showing a boy of about 10 holding a 4-inch fish hooked on a bent pin that was attached by ordinary string to a twig of a fishing pole. The boy's feet were off the ground and his face radiated ecstasy. The second panel of the cartoon depicted a middle-aged man, sour and dyspeptic, being

---

***Hugh Downs,** a distinguished television personality, is also well known as a writer, lecturer, teacher, and consultant. He is a serious student of science, music, art, literature, history, and philosophy, as well as an accomplished pilot, sailor, and racing-car driver.

photographed beside a fish larger than he was. In the background was his expensive boat and ocean-fishing gear. The cartoon required no further comment.

Where had the man lost it? Money alone would not bring him what the boy had, any more than medicine alone will bring us health. And yet money and medicine are very important.

How do we quantify happiness? I have seen cheerful hospital patients, full of hope and convalescence, regarding themselves as happy (and there is no other criterion), and I have seen affluent hypochondriacs, bitter and complaining. The sources of this happiness or unhappiness must reach far back into the early lives and backgrounds of these people.

The problem has been wrestled with over centuries by philosophers, sociologists, religious leaders, anthropologists, and psychiatrists, and all they can be certain of is that it is probably very complex. Lately, with the aid of computers, we have been able to glimpse how much more complex the problems of humanity are than we had even imagined.

Computers have thus far shown us how much we need extension of human thought processes — the very kind of extension the computers themselves provide. The question arises, "Is this self-serving on the part of the computers? Will they generate, as Jacques Ellul and some others believe, more problems than they solve?"

I incline toward a more hopeful view. My inclination is based on the history of life: it is tenacious and it moves upward. In early nature, specialization evolved and life struggled to higher levels of consciousness. Since man has appeared on the scene, whenever deep needs and problems arose, the means to fill them and cope with them somehow arose simultaneously, or at least in time to prevent the situation's unraveling. I think the appearance of the computer and technology in general is an answer to a need.

The world seems to increase in complexity. This is because our knowledge about it and ourselves as part of it becomes increasingly complicated. Our attempts to pick out general truths and rules are outstripped by accelerating change and the fast breeding of specializations.

So words like "interdisciplinary" and "synergistic" come into more frequent use because we are realizing that there is an interdependence of human issues, an ecology (if you will) of human problems: that is, they are so intricately interwoven and interdependent that it is as impossible to work on each problem in isolation from the others as it would be to remove a man's damaged liver and take it to the hospital for repair while he stayed in a bar drinking.

It is heartening to see a meeting of this kind called, and to note the keen awareness of the need to bring together a great number of disciplines and areas of concern to move meaningfully on the problem of human blight.

Environmentalists are coming to realize that if they could by magic clean the world's air and water this instant it would not stay that way without political, social, and cultural changes in man, just as medical people know that if they could give perfect health to everyone on earth right now, conditions of injustice, ignorance, and degraded environment would quickly erode it.

There are no piecemeal solutions to any of these problems. There are, in fact, no piecemeal problems. There is one overall problem: the need for a quality of life to which everyone has access, brought along by cooperation among those endowed with special knowledge and strength in each of several diverse fields. That quality of life cannot be conferred on some and withheld from others, or it will not have the vitality to be ongoing.

So the concept of quality of life is more like an organism than a machine. It has many parts, but the parts behave not merely cooperatively as in a machine, but symbiotically and sometimes holographically as in a living thing. The parts of a machine can be isolated and tested, repaired, perfected. But the components of a quality of human life are meaningful and can function only within the frame of the total concept.

Understanding this is understanding the *total* nature of the problem. This understanding has brought about this meeting. The meeting, in turn, can bring about the specific kinds of understanding that will help guide the structuring of procedures and implements to realize full human potential — the sustained, cooperative intergroup effort that alone can establish a quality of life for all.

The end product is a curious mixture of elements that cannot be guaranteed by any system but can be assumed reasonably attainable if a life has not been blighted somewhere along the way:

1. A degree of comfort with our physiological machinery and in relations with other people, institutions, and general surroundings.
2. Belief that one is loved and to a certain extent respected. Self-respect is necessary as a foundation for this.
3. Faith in one's ability to accomplish reasonable goals.
4. Challenges that produce reasonable goals, and an ongoing hope of accomplishing those goals.
5. Enough material possessions or income to provide all necessities among which is a modicum of luxury. Let's be careful how we define necessities. Oxygen is a necessity. Fresh water is a necessity. Some kind of adequate, balanced food supply, and clothing for warmth, and shelter space are necessities. Parental love and a place in a community are necessities. Luxuries are relative — an ice cream cone or a book of poetry are luxuries, just as a stable of thoroughbreds or a yacht is. Some feeling of luxury or a feeling of the right to it is essential to a life that is to have any quality. There have been lives of quality that had and needed no luxury, but this entails a degree of maturity that cannot be brought on universally by any method yet developed in human society, so we have to provide as a guarantee, a feeling of the right to acquire some degree of luxury.

6. A sense of freedom from dependency. One may depend on others — in a complex society we must depend on others — but the sense of freedom from dependency we speak of here involves participating in the decision-making apparatus of social interdependence. This must be present for a good life.

7. Ability to conform selectively — an ongoing sense of making our own decisions about when to conform and when to exert strength to change a situation (and "wisdom to know the difference").

Before listing specific issues, I want to salute the National Congress on the Quality of Life for emphasizing the foundation years in approaching the problem, and for its belief that the blighting of human lives can be prevented. Of course, efforts to remedy conditions, to alleviate suffering, to provide custodial care for the heavily blighted should continue, and such efforts deserve our praise and support. But we will never overtake the real problem of blight by any amount of remedial activity. Only by identifying conditions and events that affect life, by inaugurating actions enough in advance of the advent of individual life, and by securing the broadest possible cooperation among sectors and groups will we begin to push back the tide of suffering and waste. And a not inconsiderable by-product of success in this effort is the enormous amount of money to be saved in corrective health care, institutional care, compensatory training, special rehabilitative services, and crime control.

Quality of life must begin with health, and this involves the health of one's parents, particularly the mother, whose body provides the building materials for the first three quarters of a year after conception. If the mother is too young, or malnourished, or infected with transmissible disease, or drug addicted, the risks are high that prematurity or retardation or congenital infection or other damage will cut down completely the quality of one's life no matter what subsequent opportunities of education and environment present themselves.

Quality of the home life in early years is next. If one arrives in this world undamaged and healthy but lacks the supportive surroundings of parental love and guidance and the opportunity to grow and develop autonomy within a framework of limits set by that very love; or if one suffers the bitterness of racial discrimination or grinding poverty or both; or if the physical surroundings are dirty and dangerous, there is risk again.

If the quality of education available is poor, if one is made to feel alien and inferior because of poor teachers, outmoded concepts of schooling, and irrelevant classroom material, basic habits of thought will be forfeited and life will likely always be a little uphill from here on, no matter how fortunate circumstances might otherwise be.

If all these hurdles are cleared and adolescence is reached without too many scars, but peer-group goals are bad and natural feelings of rebellion cannot be given constructive outlets, there is still risk — risk that any real quality living will always remain just out of reach.

So there are a number of environments through and into which a human passes in becoming an adult and each of these must meet certain standards to maximize the chances for quality of life. Some of them overlap, but in sequence they are the intrauterine environment, the home environment, the school environment, the social and political environment, and the physical environment.

Our physical health and mental efficiency are highly dependent on the intrauterine environment, the first one we find ourselves in. Is the mother's body balanced, mature, healthy, sufficient in the chemicals of which we are to be made and free of chemicals and diseases that will harm us?

In the home environment we will acquire the emotional balance and nutriments of love and support that will allow growth of a sense of security and the capacity to love both ourselves and others. Does the home have a father? Does the mother have the maturity to know what to do and to care, the economic security to spend time with the child? Is a sense of identity available to the child through the model of a happy home?

The school environment is the one in which we can forge our first formal habits of thought and our first techniques for educating ourselves, through reading and learning the thoughts of others besides our teachers and parents. Is the curriculum relevant? Does the school fit our background? We cannot be expected to fit the school's background. The school must be the flexible party, but it often is completely rigid.

Meanwhile, we have also been immersed unavoidably in the socio-political and physical environments, and we will remain in these. In the first of these, we are to experience and form our attitudes toward justice, freedom, personal safety. If our larger society is oppressive, we will feel oppressed, both through sensing our parents' feelings on the matter and through direct, personal experience. If our government fails to deliver on guarantees of freedom and gives evidence of a double-standard justice — one for the rich and another for the poor — we will understandably come to believe that we are not among the franchised. We will understandably feel bitter at being deprived of something basic to a good life, and we will understandably never feel secure.

The physical environment — the air we breath, the water we drink, the food we ingest, and the temperatures we change or endure — this environment certainly factors in the quality of our living. And here there is a little less injustice than in some of the other environments: DDT accumulates in the livers of the rich as well as the poor; and an increase in the background count of radiation will not single out one race to harm. As important as this environment is, I list it last, because how we deal with it collectively will be determined largely by how safely we have come through the hazards of the other environments, particularly the very earliest. As adult individuals we can do something about our own air and food sources, and our own government. As embryos, we can do nothing about our mothers' nutrition or drug habits.

But we can do something about the fate of oncoming generations in these early environments — by enhancing conditions of nutrition, education and justice, for their parents.

There are many knowledgeable people here at this Congress — experts who know all the problems and some of the answers — people who have approaches in mind that may lead to those remaining answers. Let me give them scope by shortening my remarks. But let me wish them well and trust they will be guided at these meetings by what an unborn human might reasonably ask for himself and his future if he could.

> Whoever she is, I want my mother's body to be a fit factory for the building of my own. I want her mind to be free of oppression and able to want me and to care for me, and to love me as I will one day come to love her.
>
> Whatever race I am born to, for the sake of all races, I want my home to be secure enough that no feeling of hopelessness or myth of inferiority will be passed on to me.
>
> Whatever schooling is available to me I want the chance to learn what I will need to learn in order to grow.
>
> Under whatever kind of government I am born, I want equal justice under which I will forge my own freedom.

C.

Changing Ethics and The Quality of Life

Martin E. Marty*

According to the 16th-century British thinker Richard Hooker, "Change is not made without inconvenience, even from worse to better."[1] In our time the public gives signs that it regards itself as inconvenienced by ethical change, which it almost always sees as a movement "from better to worse."

In the modern metropolitan jungle, the increase of crime — from major felony through executive cheating — is blamed on a new ethics of permissiveness. The instability of the home and marital breakups are the result, it is said, of the new morality in the sexual realm. The quality of life of the young has deteriorated, the charge comes across the gap of generations, because young people have formulated a new ethic that repudiates old values.

The movement from "better to worse" is not our main concern, however. For one thing, the subject is covered more frequently, with little positive effect. Second, historians have great difficulty demonstrating that our times are indeed more violent, corrupt, brutal, or dishonest than were times past. It is characteristic of established generations through the ages to view their own time as one in which everything is falling apart in the hands of their oncoming successors. It must also be said that where moral decay is discernible and demonstrable, this could be seen to be a lapsing from old codes rather than living by new ones. If responses to the poll-takers in recent decades are accurate indicators, the vast majority of people in our society do conceive of themselves as still cherishing and living by older, inherited ethical systems and patterns.

More fruitful than one more inquiry about what present-day lapses tell about old codes is the pursuit of the other side of Hooker's dictum. Even the change from "worse to better," he says, can be inconveniencing. If that proves to be the case, the inconveniencing factors will have to be

*Martin E. Marty, PhD, is professor of modern church history, University of Chicago, and associate editor of The Christian Century. At the University of Chicago he is also associate dean of the divinity school, member of the faculty of the Committee on the History of Culture, and associate member of the history faculty.

appraised and faced if the quality of life is to be improved as a result of changes in ethics.

The latter years of the 20th century could see, for example, a movement of the people of the world toward a more ecumenical ideal, in which decrease of international tensions would be accompanied by a new appreciation of the whole family of man. Domestically, it can also be suggested that society is moving toward adoption of more open, acceptant interpersonal attitudes.

In both cases, a better quality of life should result from the change, since life itself would more likely be perpetuated, health and well-being enhanced, and opportunities for personal development and fulfillment enlarged under these new conditions. Yet, if these movements would mature, they would inconvenience the majority of people, since so many have heavy investments in walls and barriers, in defensive and aggressive weapons, and in habits of mind about ways of life that derive relative security from the old patterns.

Posit, then, the possibility of change from worse to better in ethical understandings; the question then rises: what would, or what does, prevent perception, appropriation, transmission, communication, and consolidation of such a change's benefits, especially so far as the young or those associated with the young are concerned?

I shall argue that change for the better is retarded in part because the public is inconvenienced insofar as (1) the habits of mind it now holds, and (2) the reconstructive energies the new situation would demand.

It is inconveniencing to be jostled in respect to one's basic perceptions of a universe, one's fundamental apprehensions of reality. For several reasons, the public's instinct, therefore, is to see any change in ethical systems to be from better to worse. At the root may be a natural sense of uncertainty as to whether the new would work better than the old, which — while it may not be serving very well — at least is time-tested. Perhaps the old pattern is perceived as having had divine sanction, or as being the result of the best efforts of honored fathers. Unless the new can be shown in advance to have similar sanctions, it is difficult for a complex society to be prepared for experiment. As Hilaire Belloc advised,

So always keep a hold on nurse
For fear of finding something worse.[2]

Whether our culture will be given the luxury of clinging to simply inherited patterns much longer is questionable. One must ask how many strains can be put on such patterns before they break; how many lapses have to occur before the framework itself is called into question; how many adaptations or transformations are possible before the original base is wholly obscured.

One sees these changes occurring, for example, in respect to what has been called, with only partial accuracy, "the Protestant Ethic." While lip service is still extended to that ethical understanding, the society is not really arranged on its basis, and thoughtful people have come to see that, if its assumptions were to be acted upon, our economy would grind to a halt. Eventually, people seek a fresh statement of an ethic for work and leisure.

Along with the uncertainty about an untested new ethic there is a natural attachment to a mythic past. In a time of chaos and shipwreck, it is understandable that people should reduce the inherited order or disorder to simple outline, and see it as part of "the good old days." The Protestant Ethic, the Old Morality in sexual matters, the American Way of Life, and similar formulations are recalled as if they had once been unchallenged in a happier world of homogeneity, simplicity, tradition, agreed-upon ground rules, discipline, and continuity. Even if not all their features are or ever were attractive, and even if our contemporaries do not choose to live by them, they did provide some groundwork. One at least knew against what one was rebelling; today, according to many, ethical anarchy prevails.

Those who enjoy such moral nostalgia usually center their reveries on three propositions about the past. First, in the past, ethics was built on absolutes, and today simple relativism prevails. An absolute value implied that it was valid under every kind of circumstance, no matter what. Lines were clearly drawn. God or human authority would enforce codes of conduct based on such absolutes. But today wishy-washy leaders let go of these absolutes.

Unfortunately, the historian of ethics cannot find such a simple pattern in the past. He can chronicle the belief held by various segregated societies that they themselves lived by universal absolutes. But modern pluralism shatters the myth of universality or consensus. The Bantus in Africa have a saying, "He who never travels thinks mother is the only cook." Modern travel and communication have assaulted the intact provincial kitchens in which people could be confident about their own absolute hold on absolutes, in their recipes for living.

A second way to put the case for a Golden Age was that "natural law" provided a consistent base for casuistry and decision. Yet here historical study also reveals only that societies claiming to be grounded in a true appropriation of natural law could not agree on the substance of that formal category. To Roman Catholics, "artificial" birth control was against natural law, and to non-Catholics it often was not. Who was to arbitrate?

This is not to say that ethics in the future will be completely disassociated from natural law, but only that assertion of its existence does not and will not resolve basic ethical disputes. It merely changes the venue or terms of debate.

Third, the good old days were also characterized by stable institutions that assured ethical continuity: the schools of old, the churches and synagogues, and, most of all, the family guaranteed that the young could develop lives of ethical quality without basic assault upon their integrities. Again, the historian cannot help but notice the relative stability of those institutions in a premodern world. However, continuity did not always

154

mean a base for good conduct. Feudal society had institutional stability and tradition to spare, and it was even grounded on a perception of divine sanctions, yet few would honestly turn to it as a prototype for human moral conduct.

My thesis to this point is emerging: *It is not likely that ethical discourse will get anywhere unless a significant number of people in a society can be prepared to experiment and to adventure.* The risk can be based on the comprehension that "what we have is not all *that* good or effective." It would be accompanied by a positive vision gained from the relativizing perspective that modern studies provide. When the mythic view of the past is questioned and the old formulation is regarded as less sacred or as irreformable, it is possible to venture.

None of this can occur, as Hooker suggested, without inconvenience. It is not easy for once-provincial people to live in an almost unsheltered pluralism. Some persons may have to learn to say, under the tutelage of men, with the late Father John Courtney Murray that such "pluralism is against the will of God. But it is the human condition; it is written into the script of history. It will not somehow marvelously cease to trouble the city."[3] That is, they may still believe in their absolutes and ultimates, but they will have to come to terms with others who do not share them. Only then is it possible for them to revise the institutions through which ethical intentions are transmitted and in which the young are nurtured.

We have not suggested that the past has nothing to say to formulators of ethics for tomorrow. Conservatives recognize this when, in the spirit of Edmund Burke, they affirm their belief that "if it is not necessary to change, it is necessary *not* to change." That is, one must work at effecting a relation between the old or inherited on one hand and the new context on the other. Effective conservatives do not just let things happen; they know that they will be changed by corrosive processes. They intervene in history to state their cases. As Carl Degler has said of the American founding fathers, "Conservatives can be innovators."

More radical innovators are equally at home with new formulations. One can turn Burke's saying around and say, "If it is necessary to change, then it is necessary *really* to change." Once again, one must work at effecting the new situation; drift offers little but anomie and anarchy. The reformer of ethics draws on terms, images, models from the past — he has no place else to go for resource — but fabricates webs that he believes will be as appropriate for a new day as old formulas or constructs were for old days.

Both sides, if they are thoughtful, will recognize that there are no foreseeable circumstances that today can abort, or even greatly retard, change and bring the society to stasis. Society will profit from their argument of competing cases, just as it suffers whenever people suspend argument, to replace it by complaint about drift and lapse. Children have little possibility of putting together believable ethical patternings in the face of those who simply permit change to occur unmonitored, uncomprehended.

Just as most of us will have to experience inconvenience to our habits of mind because ethical change is assaulting, so, too, there will be inconvenience to all who are lethargic about taking part in ethical reconstruction.

At first sight, the constructive task seems so unimaginably complicated that one is tempted to sit back. But, in my reading, which is not optimistic but in which realism is tempered with hope, it is possible to suggest that matters are not as bad as they seem, and there are at least some handles. Optimism would suggest that new ethics would "answer all the hard questions." Realism necessitates our being content with simply clarifying the basis on which hard questions are faced. Let me suggest several elements in an outline.

First, as has been implied throughout, while the new context is complicated, it is not wholly out of continuity with the past. Therefore, it is possible to draw on past ethical discourse for some guidelines. Greco-Roman, Judeo-Christian, and other lineages that are part of our tradition remain as basic resources for ethical formulation, and to these have been added resources from cultures that have been previously less familiar or even less accessible to most of us.

While the *numbers* of decisions that humans must make are infinite, the *general patterning* of their choices relate to a relatively limited set of contexts. As Talcott Parsons and Edward Shils, students of comparative cultures, point out, mere chaotic relativism need not be the only vision of the pluralist:

> There has been a tendency, under the impact of insight into the wider range of differences among cultures, to think, implicitly at least, of a limitlessly pluralistic value-universe. In its extreme form, the proponents of this view have even asserted that every moral standard is necessarily unique. There is much aesthetic sensibility underlying and justifying this contention, but it is neither convincing logically nor fruitful scientifically.[4]

If the teacher, parent, or leader and the child unite in the perception of a "limitlessly pluralistic value-universe" in which "every moral standard is necessarily unique," they will regard this to be true not only of cultures or societies but of individuals as well. Just as Dostoevski's antihero in *The Brothers Karamazov* could say, "everything is permissible" if there is no God, the young would simply weary of the pursuit of the ethical in the face of threatening or debilitating, limitless pluralism of values.

The fundamental value-issues confronting the child and his or her seniors are finally relatively few; Socrates, Jesus, Maimonides, and Spinoza — to name some examples — addressed themselves to these. There are congruences in the thought of past formulators, and their differences can be creative instead of enervating.

Another way to suggest this is that the modern decline of confidence in absolutes or natural law does not necessarily leave people shipwrecked and adrift. Too many people who have survived "the decline of the absolute" or the assault on natural law have lived on to serve as models of ethical humanity or pioneers of a rich quality of life to permit one to associate the new understandings of absolutes with simple ethical failure. R. E. Money-Kyrle posed a third alternative:

> The basis of morality is . . . neither *a priori* and universal as the metaphysicians claimed, nor empirical and relative as critical philosophers and anthropologists maintain, but empirical and universal in the sense that it is a quality, like binocular vision or an articulated thumb, which is found to be common to all mankind.[4]

Clyde Kluckhohn built on assertions such as these to come up with "two fairly cheerful propositions":

1. The similarities in human needs and human response potentialities across cultures do at any rate greatly heighten the possibilities of cross-cultural communication once these core likenesses have been somewhat disentangled from their cultural wrappings.
2. While we must not glibly equate universals with absolutes, the existence of a universal certainly raises this question: If, in spite of biological variation and historical and environmental diversities, we find these congruences, is there not a presumptive likelihood that these moral principles somehow correspond to inevitabilities, given the nature of the human organism and of the human situation? They may at any rate lead us to "conditional absolutes" or "moving absolutes," not in the metaphysical but in the empirical sense.[4]

He goes on to cite the possibly too affirmative and buoyant passage from Abraham Maslow in which these "conditional absolutes" are seen to be moving society to a better, not worse, ethical situation:

> Once granted reliable knowledge of what man *can* be under "certain-conditions-which-we-have-learned-to-call-good," and granted that he is happy, serene, self-accepting, unguilty, and at peace with himself only when he is fulfilling himself and becoming what he can be, then it is possible and reasonable to speak about good and right and bad and wrong and desirable and undesirable. . . .[4]

Such discussion may fall far short of the metaphysical hungers manifested by some who feel they cannot act unless everything is settled on a firm basis. To them it should be said that we are describing a minimal base and see no reason to inhibit their search for "more." Conditional absolutes" or "moving absolutes" are here posed over against merely bewildering citations of ethical differences on cultural and individualistic lines. They provide a circumstance in which the young can find motivation to share in formulating ethics even as their curiosity to pursue implications of cultural differences is stimulated.

Formulation and inquiry will not be sustained, however, unless significant numbers of well-placed members in society place a high premium on value-inquiry. The public as a whole may give every indication that it is in a shopping mood for values, but gifted educators, jurists, doctors, teachers, parents, and authors will have to fashion and project the symbols to which larger publics can respond.

Such projection will depend upon the creation of occasions; one way to see this is by a study of institutional changes. In the matter of institutions and value-formation of the young, the observer is likely to become aware early of a surprising situation. Whereas it is ordinarily presumed that the field of ethical or moral discourse and value-propagation among the young is crowded, everyone actually seems to be somehow backing off. The values that do come through are often proposed accidentally and not intentionally; they are then casually appropriated, though not necessarily without detrimental effect. The signals enhancing violence on television would provide a good example of this.

What institutions will take part in facing up to the issue of ethical change and the quality of life? We have just mentioned mass media of communication; they will certainly be involved. But, as William Stephenson has shown, these media meet the conditions of "convergent selectivity," advertising, and entertainment, and as such have to do chiefly with "notions, wants, images," or "fads, manners, fashions, taste, and the like." On the other hand, "social control" areas and conditions have to do with "conformity, consensus, and established custom," and relate to "opinion, attitude, and belief."

> The principle of social control is made manifest in our inner beliefs and values. It gives us our religious belief, our political faith, our status and place in life.[5]

Social control occurs in spheres closest to one's ego and is most effective during early childhood and in spheres of intimacy and inter-personality. ("Control" here is not to be taken in an authoritarian or even Orwellian sense, but rather only in contrast to "convergent selectivity" that concerns "new or non-customary modes of behavior, our fads and fancies, which allow us opportunities to exist for ourselves, to please ourselves.")

Joseph T. Klapper collated numerous empirical studies and came to the conclusion that "conversion" and formation of deepest ego-involvements occur ordinarily in areas of prolonged, intimate, personal contact, especially in the case of the child; the media tend to reinforce or confirm rather than convert or engage in formation.[6] If this is true, as I believe, it does not mean that the media are insignificant in value-formation, but that they are only one among many shaping influences and their special kinds of effects have to be comprehended if they are to be properly utilized creatively in a time of ethical change.

One would turn next, then, to children's peers: playmates, friends, siblings. They certainly belong to the area of what Stephenson called "social control," and have immeasurable impact on ethical patterning. But these peers are themselves either victims of uninterpreted ethical change or beneficiaries of monitored or intentional change.

Intentional change comes decisively through the child's schools and other educational institutions. Here the move from accidental to intentional formation has to occur in a time of ethical change. We are all aware of how delicate and dangerous this topic is and what responsibility it exacts from teachers, who have great potential for influencing children. The case of noisy reaction to discussion of values in sex education courses is only the most visible of a number of responses from a nervous or recalcitrant clientele. But, for all the diplomacy involved and for all the re-education of teachers that has to go on, it would be unthinkable to abandon controversial value discussion. There is no "no man's land." Not to discuss, one might say, is to say very much!

Take an illustration from an area second-most controversial to that of sex: religion. The majority of Americans polled were critical of the Supreme Court for throwing out time-honored values by proscribing "school prayer" in *Engel vs Vitale* and *Abington vs Schempp* in 1962 and 1963. Far from ruling them out, the court actually encouraged their reintroduction in a context more appropriate to schools, which are educational and not devotional agencies. Schools should feel free to teach about religion "and its relationship to the advancement of civilization." How this is to be done remains a subject for exploration; that it is licit and that it will inevitably relate to questions of values and ethics is evident. As the court recognized here, too, artificial silence based on proscriptions of such topics was its own kind of countercommitment.

The professions and social service agencies or voluntary associations and religious organizations are again seeing the necessity to embrace concepts of ethical change and to participate in debates toward enhancement of the quality of life. The medical profession includes an increasing number of people who call for courses on ethics in medical schools or for papers on the subject in professional journals or at professional societies. Many of the next generation's most difficult ethical questions, including what may turn out to be the most comprehensive of all — the possibility of reworking human nature through genetic tampering in the laboratories — will force systematic inquiry in the profession. The case is fairly similar for law.

Voluntary associations have special power because they are made up of people who express commitment to common basic purposes when they join such groups. Many of these associations exist, as do parallel movements, to propagate some ethical position or other. Religious organizations are often defined as inevitable participants in the ethical disputes. The question for each of these is to see whether they have become resistant to the concept of change and thus have generally abdicated responsibility for formulation and transmission of ethical argument and consequential action.

The beleaguered family most often is victim of accidental change and has few resources to withstand, interpret, innovate, or devise intentional ethics. Despite much apocalyptic talk about "the death of the family" and despite devastating assault on its serenity, the family or its equivalent will no doubt remain on the scene. If nothing is done to prepare couples before marriage or when children are expected, so that parents-to-be can eventually participate in interpreting ethical change, the children will be at the mercy of either unregulated, overwhelming change or pathetic attempts by individual families to form stays against confusion by regress to ethical frameworks that are no longer plausible.

While educators, ministers, doctors, and others assume that the family is effectively mediating ethical change, that assumption is called into question by almost every student of the modern family. All the institutions related to child-rearing seem to stand back or back off, thinking the field is crowded, while children are left at the mercy of every kind of unintegrated signal in the midst of confusing pluralism.

My remarks have been somewhat in the mood of Clyde Kluckhohn's "fairly cheerful propositions." While the situation of ethical discourse may seem to be a disaster area, I have suggested that the only hope lies in welcoming change rather than ignoring or simply resisting it; in overcoming myths of the past while retrieving what is creative from that past; in relating "conditional absolutes" to myriad contexts rather than yearning for old absolutes or wallowing in mere pluralism; in making institutional provision for change rather than leaving all to accident.

This is not the place to reinforce these suggestions by detailed discussion of the substance of new ethical theses. With Maslow (though one need not be a devoted follower of his to come to the same conclusions), one can see the possibility of "spontaneity, release, naturalness, self-acceptance, impulse-awareness, and gratification" as enhancing the quality of life, and these concepts relate to much recent ethical discourse even as they do to the "newer dynamic psychology." Our depersonalizing century has seen a new accent on the person; our period of all-embracing technology has given rise to significant numbers of people who ask how a humane technological order can develop. We have not lacked martyrs in the face of the age's terrors nor poets in the presence of its wonders. We take confidence from the men and women and children who take renewed responsibility for the care of the earth, the community, the person.

In specific subcommunities one can go much further in affirmation than this, and these subcommunities can interact to public benefit. This also ought to be said about our pluralism: In the spirit of Alfred North Whitehead, we may regard a clash of doctrines (or styles) as an opportunity and not a threat. But the opportunity can be enjoyed only if the clash occurs among mutually acceptant people. The old exclusivisms served no one, least of all children, well; such children were ill-equipped for later experiences in pluralism.

I should like to close with two illustrations. One comes from the Christian community, which has the largest residual investment in besieged ethical constructs but which, if it recovers its roots, ought to have little to fear and something to contribute to a sphere of "spontaneity, release, naturalness, self-acceptance, impulse-awareness, and gratification" or regard for earth, community, and persons. The ecumenical spirit exemplified by major figures such as Pope John XXIII has come to characterize most recent contributions to ethical formulation in the Christian sphere. Since this is the community out of which I speak, let me cite a more eloquent spokesman, the French philosopher Paul Ricoeur, on how religious particularity may relate to the universal:

> The modern world can be viewed under the twofold sign of a growing rationality along with a growing absurdity. We discover that men certainly lack justice and, most assuredly, love, but even more they lack meaning; the meaninglessness of work, leisure and sexuality. . . . Faced with these problems, our task is not one of recrimination or regret: the function of the believing community is to be a witness and representative of some fundamental meaning. . . . I do not say that others could not bear this burden; but I do say that the Christian has his own reasons for doing so. . . . The Christian stands as the adversary of the absurd and the prophet of the meaning of things. . . . He will never finish the task of spelling out and forming a complete picture of this inner meaning.[7]

This particular vision, then, is also partial, indeterminate, unfinished, and open; it has no interest in monopolies on ethical questions, but it seeks partners. It will locate them among humanists of many kinds, who might find representation in this passage by Hannah Arendt, who comments on the change in authority that relates so closely to questions of ethics and meaning:

> Authority, resting on a foundation in the past as its unshaken cornerstone, gave the world the permanence and durability which human beings need precisely because they are mortals — the most unstable and futile beings we know of. Its loss is tantamount to the loss of the groundwork of the world, which indeed since then has begun to shift, to change and transform itself with ever-increasing rapidity from one shape into another, as though we were living and struggling with a Protean universe, where everything at any moment can become almost anything else. But the loss of worldly permanence and reliability — which politically is identical with the loss of authority — does not entail, at least not necessarily, the loss of the human capacity for building, preserving, and caring for a world that can survive us and remain a place fit to live in for those who come after us.[8]

REFERENCES

1. *Saturday Review*, Feb 12, 1972, p 29.
2. *Cautionary Verses*. New York, Alfred Knopf.
3. *We Hold These Truths*. New York, Sheed & Ward, 1960, p 23.
4. The Parsons and Shils, Money-Kyrle, Kluckhohn, and Maslow quotations are taken from Ethical Relativity: *Sic et Non*, in Kluckhohn R (ed): *Culture and Behavior*. Glencoe, Ill, The Free Press, 1962, chap 16.
5. Stephenson, W: *The Play Theory of Mass Communication*. Chicago, University of Chicago Press, 1966, pp 196, 192ff.
6. *The Effects of Mass Communication*. Glencoe, Ill., The Free Press, 1960, chap II.
7. Quoted in Rahner K, SJ, (ed): *The Pastoral Approach to Atheism*. New York, Paulist Press, 1967, p 43.
8. *Between Past and Future*. Cleveland, Meridian, 1961, p 95.

D.

A Historical Perspective of the Growth and Developmenal Tasks of Today's Adolescents

Clark E. Vincent*

Accelerating social change is the most pervasive characteristic of our society. Adapting to social changes is a lifetime process for each of us in the latter half of the 20th century. Understanding the implications of current changes and charting the directions of future changes are prerequisites for those who seek to improve the quality of life for adolescents.

The challenges and problems confronting those who work with youth remind us of Auden's observation that there is a danger in lecturing on navigation while the ship is going down. Although the crises and emergencies of the moment seem at times to require all hands for the construction and maintenance of lifeboats, we need also to remember Cohen's reminder that more lives have been saved at sea through the study of astronomy than through the perfecting of lifeboats.

Obviously, both orientations are needed. My focus on the *historical* context of where we find ourselves today is an effort to provide perspective; this focus is not intended to negate the efforts and contributions of those whose efforts are literally lifesaving operations.

SOME ASSUMPTIONS

My first major assumption in charting the developmental tasks of tomorrow's youth is that the 14- to 24-year-olds of 1970 comprise the primary group to watch for trend lines. There are several reasons for this assumption.

1. This group has had from 14 to 24 years' exposure to the most permissive and affluent parental era ever experienced in this country.

*Clark E. Vincent, PhD, has been with the Bowman Gray School of Medicine since 1964, when he established the Behavioral Sciences Center for which he has served as director since 1966. This paper is from Dr. Clark E. Vincent's book, *Sexual and Marital Health: The Physician As a Consultant*, copyright © 1973 by McGraw-Hill, Inc. Used with permission of McGraw-Hill Book Company.

162

2. Our youth-oriented culture gave this age group an unprecedented amount of publicity and visibility, in part because, as birth-boom babies (1946–1957), their number (40 million) attracted the attention of business and of Madison Avenue.

3. In 1980, at ages 24 to 34, they will constitute the overwhelming majority of *parents*.

4. Many of the values and ideals espoused by this age group have emerged in a vacuum of responsibility; that is, many in this age group were sheltered to an unprecedented degree from the hard edges of financial, legal, and occupational responsibility.

5. As the older ones in this age group assume jobs and parenthood, their value statements and priorities appear to be undergoing considerable modification.

My second assumption is that the so-called *sexual* revolution is more accurately a *value* revolution. The dictum "tell it like it is" is not limited to the sexual area of life, yet somehow this appears to be the only area of debate about a so-called revolution. Why has it not been labeled a political revolution when young people (a) have been involved in voter registration of blacks in the South? (b) have traveled across country to participate in the 1968 presidential primaries? (c) have staged innumerable sit-ins and demonstrations as a means of exercising political power? (d) have effected changes in university policies regarding time-off for election campaigning? (e) have influenced the reduction of the voting age from 21 to 18 on the national level?

Why is it not labeled and debated as an economic revolution if young people have (a) negated the work ethos? (b) used food stamps and other welfare benefits while in college? (c) turned their backs on materialistic status symbols?

It would seem more accurate to speak of a value revolution in which sex is but one of many areas wherein youth has rearranged some value priorities and upended others.

A corollary of this second assumption is that professional personnel in the marriage and family-life fields tend to be out-of-date — focusing on emerging life styles, for example, at a time when these life styles are petering out. Another corollary is that personnel in the marriage and family-life fields are still struggling with whether or not they should give their approval to such emerging life styles. This brings up the curious phenomenon that young people today already have considerable sanction for such life styles. They have parental subsidy, approval of the dean of men and the dean of women, and the sanction of mass media in society.

SOME ASSUMPTIONS TO BE CHECKED

The first assumption needing examination concerns the *newness* of what we witnessed in the 1960s. The concept of a "chosen" people is certainly not new — the Hebrews of the Old Testament, the Mormons of the 19th century in this country, Hitler of the 20th century, the WASP, and the more recent hippies, black power and prison power advocates. Nor is the phenomenon of the true believer, described by Eric Hoffer in relation to the chosen people, a new one.

A second assumption to be checked is that the value revolution reflected in the current activities of some of our youth is widespread.

> The blunt truth is that academic violence and the disruption of academic freedom on the campus . . . are but six years old in this country; are to be found, in any degree whatever, on only about 100, out of 2,500 campuses; have been severe and persistent on hardly more than a dozen campuses, though admittedly major ones, and have been supported by but a tiny number of the nearly 8,000,000 students enrolled in institutions of higher learning.[1]

A survey was conducted in 1969, sponsored by the Carnegie Commission on Higher Education and reported in *The Chronicle of Higher Education* (1971),[2] that included more than 60,000 faculty members, 30,000 graduate students, and more than 70,000 undergraduates at 300 institutions. More than two thirds of the undergraduates reported that they were satisfied with student-faculty relations, their relations with other students, the quality of classroom teaching, the intellectual environment of the campus, and the college administration. This survey also reported that 62% of the students felt that other students who disrupt the functioning of a college should be expelled or suspended.

A nationwide survey conducted by the New York Institute of Life Insurance[3] in 1970, sampled the monetary attitudes of 3,000 young people 14 to 24. We hear and read much about the so-called antimaterialistic attitudes of youth today, but in this survey, when the youth were asked about the importance of money to them, 43% answered that it was either "a most important thing" or "a very important thing"; 50% said money was "moderately important" to them, and only 7% said money was "relatively unimportant" to them.

Still checking assumptions, we can also question whether sexual activity in college has increased or whether this is a reflection of differences in youngsters going to college. As recently as 1950 in this country, only 30% of the 18- to 19-year-olds and 9% of the 20- to 24-year-olds were enrolled in college. By 1969, these figures were 50% for 18- to 19-year-olds and 23% for 20- to 24-year-olds.

This increase in the total proportion of young people going to college has bearing on the 1948 finding of Kinsey that, for males 16 to 20 years of age, the total percentage of sexual outlet represented by coitus was 57% for the grade-school educated, 44% for the high-school educated, and only 10% for the college educated.[4] The ongoing debate among researchers concerning increases in premarital sex continues to provide some interesting data, including the ten-year comparative studies for 1958 to 1968 reported by Christensen[5] and by Bell and Chaskes.[6] These comparative studies indicate some increases in sexual activity, primarily for females, but do not take into account the relation of such increases to the sexual attitudes and behaviors of males and females attending college in 1958 as compared with those attending in 1968.

SOME PREDICTIONS

Sex will shift from a moral context to a predominantly health context by 1980. A number of factors are contributing to this shift, and it is possible to read into some earlier works an indication of this trend. Nearly 20 years ago, Nelson Foote's article on "Sex as Play"[7] noted, for example, that sex play and activity have very real contributions to make as developmental experiences in the process of growing up. This point, of course, has long been made by therapists and is implicit, if not explicit, in many current writings on evaluating premarital as well as extramarital sexual experiences. The criteria increasingly applied are mental, emotional, and physical health factors, with more attention paid to the *process* of intercoursing than to the *act* of intercourse.

This shift to a health context is central in the work of Kirkendall,[8] as it is in A. H. Maslow's discussions of love and sex between self-actualizing or healthy people. We may also note in passing the degree to which sex education and health education have combined, and the health-sex implications of current research on, for example, population problems, venereal disease, eugenics, and homosexuality.

A second prediction for 1980 is that (in part due to the women's liberation movement) finally we will begin to get to the nitty-gritty of sex education in the public schools — not the anatomy and physiology, but the psychology, sociology, philosophy, and history of maleness and femaleness. As the definition "masculinity is superiority" is discarded, what, then, is masculinity?

A third prediction is that the 14- to 24-year-olds of 1970, who will be the 24- to 34-year-olds in 1980 will, as young adults, usher in a restrictive parental era (restrictive by health rather than by moral criteria). Before considering some of the bases for this prediction, I want to consider some of the sources of the anxiety being experienced today by parents in the caught generation — those people 35 to 55 years of age.

THE CAUGHT GENERATION

Many of the 35- to 55-year-old parents of today's 14- to 24-year-olds belong to the *caught generation* — caught in between the demands of youth and the expectations of the elderly. Many of you were taught to accept and respect the authoritative (not authoritarian) wisdom and experience of your parents, but may find your own parental authority openly defied and your way of life derided.

You learned early the dignity of work, the necessity of saving. Now, you are locked into the pattern of working and attempting to save, partly by habit, but also by the two generations on either side of you. For the older generation, you may feel an obligation to backstop the dwindling resources of retired persons, whose leisure time makes your visits seem too infrequent and your work habits compulsive. For the younger generation — your children in their late teens and early twenties — you may continue to provide a least the necessities of life, while they criticize your work ethos that makes it possible for them to do their thing.

The threat of "love withdrawal," used by your parents to keep you in line as a child, may now be used by your children to keep you in line as a parent. As a child, you were to be seen and not heard; now as a parent you may feel you are to be neither seen nor heard.

Your age group, already thinned by the low birthrate during the depression and further depleted by World War II, is insufficient in numbers to fill all of the leadership roles and administrative positions usually assumed by those in their 40s and 50s. And, on each side of you are the elderly and the young whose needs and wants have increased markedly the demands on you for taxes, leadership, and administrative responsibility.

It is not surprising that some of you have stepped off the escalator — have declined the next promotion to additional administrative duties, higher taxes and a heavier work load — thus further depleting the ranks of your generation.

Your generation is suffering the painful and frequently bewildering side effects of change, of a combination of historical factors that may never be repeated. Your empathic commiseration with youth, who are confronted by a rapidity of social change that outpaces all but the very swift, is seldom reciprocated. Obscured or ignored is your own confrontation with change, with the attendant anxiety of having obsolete skills and knowledge, and insufficient time and energy to unlearn and relearn.

In essence, the caught generation is a scared generation, afraid even of its children. Such fear is denied by some, who may have resolved their anxiety about their children and their own ambivalence about their adult roles by joining, eulogizing, and subsidizing youth. Occasionally, they are the ones who "methinks doth protest too much" in defense of the hippy-types to cover their more secret fear of failure as parents of hippies. And some of them may be the ones who, stalled on the academic or business promotion ladder, encourage and use youth to attack the establishment they themselves fear. Some of them may even mimic the limited vocabulary and myopic historical view of militant youths by equating, for example, the actions of those at the Boston tea party with the destruction of property by a few of our militant youths. There is a difference: the youth of colonial times defied taxation without representation; those few of today's youth who resort to violence and destruction want representation without taxation.

Historical Perspective

For a quarter of a century, we have witnessed an unprecedented empathy for the problems, anxieties, and identity quests of youth. Writings and podium pronouncements have pressured, cajoled, and scolded parents to listen to, understand, and communicate with their teen-agers. Absent, and seldom noted as missing, have been those printed and spoken words that might have alerted youth to the necessity of reciprocity in communication. After hours of listening to youth and then being faulted for not listening, you may have realized belatedly that they equated listening with agreement; since you didn't agree with them, you obviously were not listening.

That the younger generation lacks a sense of history is hardly surprising. They were tantalized by vulgarized versions of the "here and now" of existentialism during the *sensate sixties*. They have been nurtured for two decades (1945 to 1965) on the childrearing philosophy of "fun morality." They are unaware that 20, 30, and 40 years ago, we too basked in the fleeting glory provided by our high school and college commencement speakers who, traditionally apologizing for the sorry world adults had bequeathed us, exuded confidence that we would set the world right.

Without a Pisgah perspective (the mount from which Moses viewed the Promised Land he was never to enter), the youth absorbed by the sponge-label "hippies" cannot be expected to know the disillusionment of those associated with the religious reform movements of 1830–1880, who preached and practiced almost everything advocated and tried by the hippies. The here-and-now fixation of the hippies precludes an awareness of some of the earlier religious reform movements in the United States that embraced peculiar speech and clothing, refusal to cut hair or shave beards, the sharing of sex partners, polygamy, polyandry, and a disavowal of private property. The members of these reform movements did not have drugs, but they had their "mind-expanding" visions, their "speaking in tongues,", and interpretations thereof. Many of these earlier religious reform movements gradually made 180-degree transitions from communal property to private property and vigorous capitalism, and from democratic consensus to an authoritarian hierarchy. Espousing a here-and-now cause, the hippies cannot be expected to have learned the lessons of history.

There Are No Guarantees

Their parents' degree of sympathy and empathy with young people confronted by a world of uncertainties has further aided and abetted their historical focus on the here and now. Have parents in their 40s and 50s so completely forgotten their uncertainties as youth in the 1930s? They were given no guarantee of jobs, of adequate medical care, or even the daily necessities that were dependent on father's day-to-day employment. Reared on these uncertainties and on mealtime discussions of economic bleakness, theirs were the uncertainties of Hitler's rise to power, the bombing of Pearl Harbor, and the entry into a war that appeared to be a losing proposition for two years and was expected to last at least five to ten years before (and if) we won it. Yet such uncertainties were not acceptable excuses for copping out.

The early settlers and pioneers could have used the uncertainties of being alive tomorrow or of not having sufficient food for the winter as excuses to disengage. The youth of the Civil War period could have used the lack of a national consensus as an excuse for not participating in a war in which the enemy all too frequently was a father, son, or brother.

This is not to argue that young people should be involved in Vietnam, nor to justify the United States' involvement in any war; it is to emphasize that uncertainties are part and parcel of human life, and that parents' overempathy with young people's confrontation with uncertainty has abetted youth's unrealistic expectations of guarantees.

The Perfectionist Myth

Parents in the 35-to-55 age group could never relax in childrearing as did *their* parents, who were able to get off the hook by reference to the "black sheep of the family." The parents of today's youth rarely use this phrase because of an unlimited faith in science, or what Bossard has referred to as the "philosophy of the modern mind."

Having successfully applied scientific methods in the technological revolution, our country then applied scientific methods to the study of human relations generally and childrearing specifically. Middle-class parents in particular have been indoctrinated with the notion that unless they are obtuse, evil, or stupid, it is possible to rear the perfect child. This indoctrination placed tremendous pressure on the parents, resulting in considerable feelings of guilt for failure to meet unrealistic expectations.

Confronted by teen-agers and youth who insist on a series of rights and privileges together with permissiveness, parents are doubly defeated by feelings of failure when subscribing to the notion that they should have been able to rear close-to-perfect children. Missing is the precious freedom to err. The experts themselves, of course, exercise this freedom, as is evident in the 180-degree changes in their advice. However, parents are unaware of these 20- to 30-year changes because they read the literature only when they are parents.

When Are They Launched and by Whom?

The built-in expectation that adequate parents should rear problem-free children fosters the parental inability to ever quite give up and launch their children. Thus we increasingly see the pattern of today's parents continuing to make sacrifices to support their married children in college, even when those married children have two or three children of their own. The guilt fostered in parents by the experts is felt deeply. Parents try to compensate for their purported failure by continually helping their children. It would be far more reassuring to parents were they to accept the fact that one can never really know how youngsters will turn out. Some are models of behavior at 20, and a mess at 40. Others seem hopeless at 20, and are pillars of society at 35.

Parents have been indoctrinated to assume too much credit, and hence too much blame, for their influence upon their children. There are many fingers in the pie. Between the ages of 6 and 18, most of the child's waking time is spent in contact with or under the supposed supervision of adults *other than his parents.* Madison Avenue has not only a finger but almost an entire hand in the pie, as it recognizes the tremendous buying power of youth, and addresses them as if they had both adult bodies and adult budgets.

The Inevitable Insatiability of Us All

Household pets are insatiable. One can never provide them with enough love and attention. So it is with children. The more affection, money, candy, and privileges they are given, the more they will want. Oddly enough, we act as if they will draw a line. They will not. As adults, we too are insatiable. Regardless of how much power, money, or prestige we have, most of us probably would accept more if someone would provide it. The failure to recognize the insatiability of pets, youth, and adults traps today's parents into thinking that young people will set limits on their own demands. And because of their anxiety, today's parents too frequently are more concerned with being accepted or popular with their children than with being respected.

The deliberate and tactical exploitation of adults' naivete about the insatiability of rebellious youth is clearly stated by Jerry Rubin, the self-appointed spokesman for the yippies. "Satisfy our demands, and we got twelve more, the more demands you satisfy, the more we got.[9]"

Why Today's Parents Run (Scared)

The concept that "the child is Father to the Man," stated poetically by Wordsworth and developed insightfully by Erickson,[10] is highly relevant. The essence of this concept is that, because every adult was once a child, small in physical size, in power, and in influence, the fear of again being small and impotent is forever with us, not too far below the conscious level. Hence, our adult years are permeated with repeated assertions and numerous buttresses against ever again being small, impotent, and powerless.

The teen-ager, with abundant energy, new knowledge, untarnished dreams, and idealism confronts the parents with the realities of his or her own limited energy, obsolete knowledge, unfulfilled dreams, and realistic compromise. Such confrontation reawakens our early childhood anxieties of becoming once again small, powerless, and uninfluential. Because of this, parents may overreact in attempts to exert control and influence over their teen-agers to disprove their own growing sense of impotency. For this reason — but not for this reason alone — many of today's 35- to 55-year-old parents do indeed run scared.

If we accept the psychological dictum that the frightened or insecure child needs, not less, but *more* emotional support, understanding, and love, *and if parents are people too,* then it should be readily apparent that the parents of today need, not less, but more support, encouragement, and self-confidence. Confronted by a generation of children reared by the experts' dicta on permissiveness, and inculcated with a sense of accountability for every act of misbehavior on the part of their children, parents' waning self-confidence is compounded by prolonged responsibility without authority at a time when they are outnumbered and outmaneuvered by their own teenagers. *The dignity of parenthood needs to be regained.*

All too frequently, therapists and marriage counselors see and hear of the heartache, the emotional and psychic prices being exacted from parents in the 35-to-55 age group who are bowed down with remorse, if not guilt, about their "failure as parents." And much too often, physicians see and hear the visceral and somatic, as well as psychic, price exacted from parents — particularly mothers — in this age group whose sense of failure where their children are concerned manifests itself symptomatically in a variety of functional bodily ailments that defy treatment.

This should not be! The overwhelming majority of these mothers have done a commendable job of rearing their children. Inadvertently, they are victims of a series of social and historical factors. Moreover, their sense of failure, or at least anxiety about their success as mothers, compounds the negative aspects of their relations with their daughters. They tend to become interfering grandmothers and mothers-in-law in a last effort to rectify what they have been led to believe were considerable inadequacies in their own mother role.

Youth will respect their parents *only to the degree that parents respect themselves.* Parenthood is not a popularity contest, yet the fusion of needs and wants has placed youth in the saddle to the extent that it is now youth rather than parents who threaten to withdraw and withhold love unless their wishes are granted.

TOMORROW'S PARENTS: THE PENDULUM SWINGS

What of tomorrow's parents? The current one-sided emphasis on youth has ill-prepared them for the abrupt transition to the role of parent at ages 19, 23, or 25. Better that they not be further encouraged to undermine their future role as parents by continuing the one-sided emphasis on understanding, listening to, and acceding to youth. Rather the emphasis on youth's wants, needs, and uncertainties should be balanced by a more realistic awareness of their responsibility for listening to and understanding some of the identity problems and anxieties confronting their parents.

Moreover, and perhaps a dubious consolation to the caught generation, it is my thesis that the "generation" of 14- to 24-year-olds in 1970 (the 24- to 34-year-olds in 1980) will, as they become parents, usher in during the *security-conscious seventies,* a highly restrictive childrearing era, and also a period of political conservatism and international isolationism. This thesis derives in part from the pendulum theory of history which posits that the momentum required to swing us in one direction along the arc usually carries us far beyond the intended goal, setting the stage for the return swing of the pendulum.

The wide, pendulum swings in childrearing theories and practices during the first half of this century were documented in an earlier content analysis of more than 800 professional articles and books on infant care published between 1890 and 1950.[11] The basic trends of these changes were also documented independently by Stendler[12] in a separate content analysis of three women's magazines. The trends shown for 1950–1970 are based on my more cursory review of the literature, and the trend for 1970–1980 is a projection.

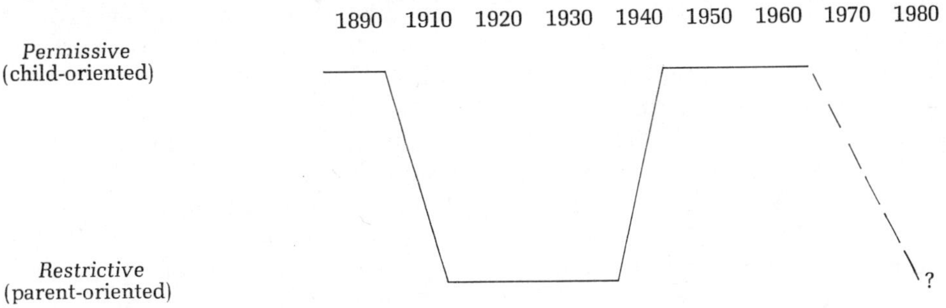

Figure 1. Childrearing trends

The period from 1915 to 1935 represented a "parents' era," with the emphasis on mother's competence and right to make decisions concerning when, where, and how her children's *needs* would be met. Obviously, not all experts, and certainly not all parents, shifted from permissive to restrictive to permissive at the same time or to the same degree. The focus here is on broad historical trends.

The extreme of the restrictive era occurred in the mid-20s. In 1923, the Children's Bureau of the United States Department of Labor was recommending, through its publication *Infant Care*, that mothers feed their infants on strict, regular schedules, and was advising that: "Toilet training may be begun as early as the end of the first month. . . . The first essential in bowel training is absolute regularity.[13(pp42-43)]" In 1928, John B. Watson was writing: "There is a sensible way of treating children. . . . Let your behavior always be objective and kindly firm. Never hug and kiss them, never let them sit in your lap. If you must, kiss them once on the forehead when they say goodnight. Shake hands with them in the morning.[14(p76)]"

The period from 1945 to 1965 represented the "children's era" that witnessed the fusion of wants with needs, the emergence of "fun morality." What the child *wanted* was presumed, even by nutritionists, to be what was needed, and therefore should be provided. In the early 40s, mothers were being advised that toilet training should not start too early or be too strict, and that "unvarying obedience is not desirable.[15(pp 45, 125)]" "It is reasonable to feed a baby when he's hungry. . . . It is unreasonable to make him wait. . . . Studies of so-called spoiled children and their homes have shown that

172

they were denied adequate mothering. [16(pp92,110)]" Beginning in the late 40s and continuing throughout the 50s and early 60s, "momism" and *cherchez la mère* became thematic.

The implications of these broad and highly generalized swings of the pendulum are as follows:

Today's 35- to 55-year-old parents were born and reared during the restrictive "parents' era" of 1915–1935. They were strongly influenced by the economic depression and the work-and-save ethic of the 1930s. However, they became and were parents during the permissive "children-youth era" of 1945–1965, which they helped to initiate and support as a reaction to the way they were reared, and which they compounded by wanting to provide their children with material advantages that they had been denied during the depression and that the affluence of the 1960s made possible.

Tomorrow's parents, the 14- to 24-year-olds in 1970, were born and reared during the permissive "children-youth era" of 1945–1965. They are accustomed to having their wants regarded as needs to be satisfied here and now. However, as parents during the 70s and 80s, they will usher in another restrictive "parents' era," consistent with their experience of having a high priority given to their own needs and wants, and consistent with their emphasis, if not insistence, upon being heard and doing their thing.

The early clues that the 14- to 24-year-olds in 1970 will usher in a restrictive "parents' era," and a conservative and isolationist era in politics, are diverse and inferential. We have the hippie commune parents whose "true-believer" fixation on doing their own thing minimizes, if not ignores, the importance of birth certificates and adequate pre- and post-natal health care for their children. On college campuses, there are those couples whose eqalitarian, experimental living together tends to crumble, reverting to more traditional forms, when they find that sharing the same pad includes the realities of making time commitments to each other and assuming financial responsibility for each other in the absence of a subsidy from one or both sets of parents.

There are those college students who are becoming righteously indignant and very outspoken about the immaturity of youth, as the college drug scene and demonstration activities shift increasingly to the high school campuses. High school students have long followed and sought to mimic college students — whether it be courtship patterns, band uniforms, student government, or the current demonstration and protest activities. The early 1970s have witnessed a greater increase in demonstrations and protests on high school campuses than on college campuses. And few things dampen the ardor of college students for a given behavior faster than the emulation of that behavior by those younger than they.

Much of the 14- to 24-year-olds' emphasis on liberality, love, sharing, and antimaterialism has flourished during the late 1960s without the reality-testing of responsibilities. Some of those youths in their early 20s who are beginning to support themselves are already complaining about paying too much income tax to support the freeloaders.

Former students, who once denounced any form of grading system, are reverting to a more traditional competitive system when they select a physician or a mechanic on the basis of his performance and authoritative knowledge rather than on pass-or-fail criteria. They also reflect the traditional competitive system when they do comparison shopping, and seek promotions or salary increases on the basis of their own individual work performance.

Another inferential clue to the advent of a restrictive parents' era is found in the comment of today's youth that their parents "couldn't control" or "lost control of them." What the 35- to 55-year-old parents perceived as being lenient and understanding, if not permissive, their college-age children perceive increasingly as being weak, ambivalent, and not in control. Given their perception, they are already commenting on their intent to change this — to maintain control, to be in charge of those younger (even by a few years) than they.

A Mistake Revisited

That youth should be heard is now a demand within almost every social institution. It includes youth's demands for a voice in the running of universities, medical schools, and city councils. It is a basic and sound principle that ideas, criticisms, and innovative suggestions should be heard and considered on the basis of their merits, rather than on the basis of whether they are presented by the young or the old, the blacks or the whites, the affluent or the poor, the experienced or the inexperienced. Youth has rightly faulted the older generation for ignoring this principle.

However, youth's insistence upon being heard and listened to by those older and more experienced than they is not matched with an equal concern that these same young people listen to and hear those younger and less experienced than they are. They demand to be heard and represented, for example, on committees of universities. But have they been equally concerned about having senior high school students represented on college-student government committees? Where are the undergraduate representatives on graduate-student committees? High school seniors will be affected for four years by changes in college-student government policies brought about by college seniors who are graduating and leaving. But to ask college students about listening to high school students is to hear them give various reasons why it wouldn't work (the difficulty of selecting a representative high school senior, the inexperience and immaturity of high school students) — reasons which they themselves readily reject when expressed by college administrators.

We ill-serve youth by acceding to their demands to be heard and represented in the councils and committees of those who are much older and far more experienced than they if we do not insist that they be willing to listen to those who are only a little younger and less experienced than they are. Youth's one-way focus on their being heard and represented is self-perpetuating in a way that can lead them not only to repeat but also to compound our mistake of not listening. At 30 they still may be more intent on being heard by those who are 40 than on listening to those who are 20. By failing to practice what they preach and demand, some young people are undermining the very principle they are espousing.

I have written as if there were only one group, one type of young person. Obviously there are almost infinite variances in the types and groupings of both youths and adults. The vast majority of our youth think, act, and live in ways that deserve our respect and admiration, but this is equally true of the vast majority of the caught generation of 35- to 55-year-old parents.

If my predictions are even partially correct, there is real cause for concern that the pendulum swing toward a restrictive-conservative era is moving much too rapidly. A major implication of such a pendulum swing is that efforts to improve the quality of life for children and youth in the late 1970s and early 1980s should not assume a unilinear extension of today's parental and societal permissiveness.

A closely related phenomenon is the impatience of today's youth, which may or may not mean they will be impatient as parents in 1980. The parents of today's youth learned patience, for example, during the depression when the scarcity of jobs necessitated they be very patient and forebearing of any injustices on the part of one's employer, as well as patient about effecting changes in the system or establishment. Such patience is viewed as weakness or even hypocrisy by many of today's youth who were reared on action and demonstrations demanding instant change in the establishment. To the degree youth has been praised by their peers for demanding instant change in their elders or in authority figures, they find it hard to be patient with each other as marital partners — wanting the spouse to change *now*. Will they show the same impatience with their children?

For those of you in the caught generation, there is the consolation that your grandchildren will be more respectful, appreciative, and well-mannered.

REFERENCES

1. Nisbet RA: The counter-culture and its apologists: I. *Commentary*, Dec 1970, pp 40–45.

2. Carnegie Commission on Higher Education: *The Chronicle of Higher Education*, vol 5, no 15, Jan 18, 1971.

3. New York Institute of Life Insurance: Finance Related Attitudes of Youth: 1970. Division of Statistics and Research, 1971.

4. Kinsey AC, Pomeroy WD, Martin CB: *Sexual Behavior in the Human Male*. Philadelphia, WB Saunders, 1948.

5. Christensen HT, Gregg CF: Changing sex norms in America and Scandinavia. *Journal of Marriage and the Family* 32: 616–627, Nov 1970.

6. Bell RE, Chaskes JD: Premarital sexual experience among coeds, 1958 and 1968. *Journal of Marriage and the Family* **32**: 81–84, Feb 1970.

7. Foote N: Sex as play. *Social Problems* **1**: 159–163, April 1953.

8. Kirkendall L: *Premarital Intercourse and Interpersonal Relationships.* New York, Julian Press, 1961.

9. Rubin J: *Do It.* New York, Simon and Schuster, 1970.

10. Erickson EH: The problem of ego identity. *J Am Psychoanal Assoc* **4:** 52–121, 1956. *Childhood and Society.* New York, WW Norton, 1963.

11. Vincent CE: Trends in infant care. *Child Dev* **22**: 199–209, Sept 1951.

12. Stendler CB: Sixty years of child-training practices. *J Pediatr* **36:** 122–136, 1950.

13. US Department of Labor, Children's Bureau: *Infant Care.* Washington DC, Government Printing Office, 1923.

14. Watson JB: *Psychological Care of Infant and Child.* London, Allen and Unwin, 1928.

15. Bradbury EE, Amidon EP: *Learning to Care for Children.* New York, Appleton-Century, 1943.

16. Kenyon J: Less rigid schedules for baby. *Good Housekeeping,* 1940, pp 92–110.